BETH DANA

MAKE

MONEY

YOUR

PARTNER

Quarterly Financial Goal Tracker,

Planner & Journal

Make Money Your Partner:
Quarterly Financial Goal Tracker, Planner & Journal

ISBN: 978-1-63972-344-7

Printed in the U.S.A.

Cover Design: Jessica George

www.bethldana.com

WELCOME

The 'Make Money Your Partner' series continues!

This *Quarterly Financial Goal Tracker, Planner & Journal* is designed to serve as your guide towards creating the life of your dreams. Many of you have completed the 'Make Money Your Partner' 30-day guides, and are ready to take your journey to the next level, and this will support you in achieving your next level of success. Thank you for choosing to lead in designing the life of your dreams.

Let the journey begin! With Love & Gratitude,

Beth

"Financial Health is Restored in two ways -first by doing the INNER WORK of how you think and feel about money and then by doing the OUTER WORK of Practical Money Management."

- Marianne Williamson

BUDGET FORMULA

The following is a recommended budget formula which can help you as you begin moving towards creating healthy money habits and fostering financial freedom. A common mistake people make is they first spend money, then they save. When this happens, most of their money is spent, leaving little to nothing to save. Here we will focus on the bigger picture: what money is and how it can be focused in the right direction, to ultimately attract more money and peace of mind.

Money Allocation

10% Donating/Tithing

When we focus on giving to the world, we create the flow of abundance. We must give for the sake of giving, without attachment or expectation. When we are in the state of abundance, our vibration rises and we are confident that we are and will be taken care of. Contribute to charities and organizations that make a difference in areas that you are passionate about.

20% Saving

- The first type of saving you should be doing is Long-Term Saving. This is your retirement fund. This is your #1 savings area. If you don't focus on your long-term savings, you'll never get there.

- Next is Mid-Term Saving. This is your fund for large purchases such as a new car, new home, etc.

- Finally, Short-Term Saving. This is your safety fund. This is 3-6 months' worth of your income. You may never actually reach this full amount as your safety fund is designed for money to be constantly going in and out. It's for unexpected events such as travel, gifts, car repairs, leaky roof, etc.

30% Living Expenses

This is your monthly living and household expenses.

40% Rent/Mortgage

This is your monthly rent or mortgage expense.

DAILY GUIDE

Morning Routine
Start with any amount of stretching and/or exercising, prayer, and meditation that feels comfortable for you, building this over time until you reach a routine that feels right. This session will bring into alignment your mind, body and spirit.

Read/Audio
Read or listen to an audio book for a minimum of 30 minutes per day. Read books that are positive, uplifting, feed your soul, and are forwarding in your goals.

Intention
Set your intention for the day; what are you committed to creating? This might be a larger goal of yours, or just a way of living and acting towards yourself and others. It's your commitment for the day. Let it be true for you and act on it with purpose and integrity.

Word of the Day
This word is a message that will guide you through your day. It can be a word that calls to you intuitively, or you can use angel cards. The word may not resonate with you at first, but be mindful of it throughout the day and take notice as a lesson and focus on why that word is so significant.

Affirmation
An affirmation is a statement which you aspire to be in life. You are speaking into existence the person you want to become.

Gratitude
What are you grateful for? Living with gratitude opens the pathways to abundance. It is the highest vibration we can be in. List people and/or things that you are grateful for each day.

Read Monthly Declarations
Being connected to our declarations is powerful in creating and manifesting. As life and circumstances happen we can sometimes lose sight of our goals and dreams, so to stay connected. I invite you to read your monthly declarations every day, being reminded to focus your time and energy on what is most important to you.

To-Do's
In this section you will write your to-do list for the day. Take notice of what you focus your time and energy on. Are these things aligned with your declarations?

People to Contact
Make a list of people you want to connect with. These can be a combination of business and personal connections. The beauty is in the connecting.

Expenses & Investing/Saving
Take time to really connect with and be aware of your daily expenses. As money comes in, notice where and how you spend money and how you invest it. Use this daily information to complete your monthly tracker.

Daily Schedule
Pre-planning our day is valuable in creating structure in accomplishing the goals we set for ourselves. Spend the evening before pre-planning your next day.

QUARTER DECLARATIONS

What do you want to achieve in all areas of your life in the next 3 months?

Faith/Spirituality:

- ....
- ....
- ....

Mindset/Personal   Development:

- ....
- ....
- ....

Family/Relationships:

- ....
- ....
- ....

Health/Fitness:

- ....
- ....
- ....

Business/Career:

- ....
- ....
- ....

Community/Contribution:

- ....
- ....
- ....

Money/Finances:

- ....
- ....
- ....

I, (full name) ....

declare to accomplish the above handwritten goals in excellence by (date) ....

Month

MONTHLY EXPENSE TRACKER

Date	Expense Category	Budget	Actual
	Donating/Tithing		
	Living Expenses		
	Rent/ Mortgage		
Total		$	$

MONTHLY INCOME & SAVINGS TRACKER

Date	Income	Savings/ Investing	Account
Total	$	$	

MONTHLY NOTES / JOURNAL

MONTHLY DECLARATIONS

What do you want to achieve in all areas of your life this month?

Faith/Spirituality:

- _____
- _____
- _____

Mindset/Personal   Development:

- _____
- _____
- _____

Family/Relationships:

- _____
- _____
- _____

Health/Fitness:

- _____
- _____
- _____

Business/Career:

- _____
- _____
- _____

Community/Contribution:

- _____
- _____
- _____

Money/Finances:

- _____
- _____
- _____

I, (full name) _____

declare to accomplish the above handwritten goals in excellence by (date) _____

DAILY TRACKER

Date_____

Intention:_____

Affirmation:_____

Word of the Day:_____

7 :00	
:30	
8 :00	
:30	
9 :00	
:30	
10 :00	
:30	
11 :00	
:30	
12 :00	
:30	
1 :00	
:30	
2 :00	
:30	
3 :00	
:30	
4 :00	
:30	
5 :00	
:30	
6 :00	
:30	
7 :00	
:30	
8 :00	
:30	
9 :00	
:30	
10 :00	
:30	

• Exercise/Stretches: _____ mins

• Pray/Meditation: _____ mins

• Read/Audio: _____ mins

I am reading /listening to:

_____

I Am Grateful for:

• _____

• _____

• _____

• _____

• _____

☐ I read my Monthly Declarations

To-Do's:

☐ _____

☐ _____

☐ _____

☐ _____

☐ _____

People to Contact:

☐ _____

☐ _____

☐ _____

☐ _____

☐ _____

Expenses: Investing/ Saving:

Item	Amount	Item	Amount

DAILY TRACKER

Date ....

Intention: ....
Affirmation: ....
Word of the Day: ....

7 :00	
:30	
8 :00	
:30	
9 :00	
:30	
10 :00	
:30	
11 :00	
:30	
12 :00	
:30	
1 :00	
:30	
2 :00	
:30	
3 :00	
:30	
4 :00	
:30	
5 :00	
:30	
6 :00	
:30	
7 :00	
:30	
8 :00	
:30	
9 :00	
:30	
10 :00	
:30	

• Exercise/Stretches: .... mins
• Pray/Meditation: .... mins
• Read/Audio: .... mins

I am reading /listening to:

_____

I Am Grateful for:

• ....
• ....
• ....
• ....
• ....

☐ I read my Monthly Declarations

To-Do's:
☐ ....
☐ ....
☐ ....
☐ ....
☐ ....

People to Contact:
☐ ....
☐ ....
☐ ....
☐ ....
☐ ....

Expenses: Investing/ Saving:

Item	Amount	Item	Amount

DAILY TRACKER

Date ....

Intention: ....

Affirmation: ....

Word of the Day: ....

7 :00	
:30	
8 :00	
:30	
9 :00	
:30	
10 :00	
:30	
11 :00	
:30	
12 :00	
:30	
1 :00	
:30	
2 :00	
:30	
3 :00	
:30	
4 :00	
:30	
5 :00	
:30	
6 :00	
:30	
7 :00	
:30	
8 :00	
:30	
9 :00	
:30	
10 :00	
:30	

- Exercise/Stretches: .... mins
- Pray/Meditation: .... mins
- Read/Audio: .... mins

I am reading /listening to:

_____

I Am Grateful for:
- ....
- ....
- ....
- ....
- ....

☐ I read my Monthly Declarations

To-Do's:
- ☐ ....
- ☐ ....
- ☐ ....
- ☐ ....
- ☐ ....

People to Contact:
- ☐ ....
- ☐ ....
- ☐ ....
- ☐ ....
- ☐ ....

Expenses: Investing/ Saving:

Item	Amount	Item	Amount

DAILY TRACKER

Date ....

Intention: ....
Affirmation: ....
Word of the Day: ....

7 :00	
:30	
8 :00	
:30	
9 :00	
:30	
10 :00	
:30	
11 :00	
:30	
12 :00	
:30	
1 :00	
:30	
2 :00	
:30	
3 :00	
:30	
4 :00	
:30	
5 :00	
:30	
6 :00	
:30	
7 :00	
:30	
8 :00	
:30	
9 :00	
:30	
10 :00	
:30	

- Exercise/Stretches: .... mins
- Pray/Meditation: .... mins
- Read/Audio: .... mins

I am reading /listening to:

_____

I Am Grateful for:
- ....
- ....
- ....
- ....
- ....

☐ I read my Monthly Declarations

To-Do's:
☐ ....
☐ ....
☐ ....
☐ ....
☐ ....

People to Contact:
☐ ....
☐ ....
☐ ....
☐ ....
☐ ....

Expenses: Investing/ Saving:

Item	Amount	Item	Amount

DAILY TRACKER

Date ....

Intention: ....
Affirmation: ....
Word of the Day: ....

7 :00	
:30	
8 :00	
:30	
9 :00	
:30	
10 :00	
:30	
11 :00	
:30	
12 :00	
:30	
1 :00	
:30	
2 :00	
:30	
3 :00	
:30	
4 :00	
:30	
5 :00	
:30	
6 :00	
:30	
7 :00	
:30	
8 :00	
:30	
9 :00	
:30	
10 :00	
:30	

- Exercise/Stretches: .... mins
- Pray/Meditation: .... mins
- Read/Audio: .... mins

I am reading /listening to:

_____

I Am Grateful for:
- ....
- ....
- ....
- ....
- ....

☐ I read my Monthly Declarations

To-Do's:
☐ ....
☐ ....
☐ ....
☐ ....
☐ ....

People to Contact:
☐ ....
☐ ....
☐ ....
☐ ....
☐ ....

Expenses: Investing/ Saving:

Item	Amount	Item	Amount

DAILY TRACKER

Date ....

Intention: ....

Affirmation: ....

Word of the Day: ....

7 :00		
:30		
8 :00		
:30		
9 :00		
:30		
10 :00		
:30		
11 :00		
:30		
12 :00		
:30		
1 :00		
:30		
2 :00		
:30		
3 :00		
:30		
4 :00		
:30		
5 :00		
:30		
6 :00		
:30		
7 :00		
:30		
8 :00		
:30		
9 :00		
:30		
10 :00		
:30		

- Exercise/Stretches: .... mins
- Pray/Meditation: .... mins
- Read/Audio: .... mins

I am reading /listening to:

_____

I Am Grateful for:

- ....
- ....
- ....
- ....
- ....

☐ I read my Monthly Declarations

To-Do's:

☐ ....
☐ ....
☐ ....
☐ ....
☐ ....

People to Contact:

☐ ....
☐ ....
☐ ....
☐ ....
☐ ....

Expenses: Investing/ Saving:

Item	Amount	Item	Amount

DAILY TRACKER

Date ....

Intention: ....
Affirmation: ....
Word of the Day: ....

7 :00	
:30	
8 :00	
:30	
9 :00	
:30	
10 :00	
:30	
11 :00	
:30	
12 :00	
:30	
1 :00	
:30	
2 :00	
:30	
3 :00	
:30	
4 :00	
:30	
5 :00	
:30	
6 :00	
:30	
7 :00	
:30	
8 :00	
:30	
9 :00	
:30	
10 :00	
:30	

- Exercise/Stretches: .... mins
- Pray/Meditation: .... mins
- Read/Audio: .... mins

I am reading /listening to:

_____

I Am Grateful for:
- ....
- ....
- ....
- ....
- ....

☐ I read my Monthly Declarations

To-Do's:
☐ ....
☐ ....
☐ ....
☐ ....
☐ ....

People to Contact:
☐ ....
☐ ....
☐ ....
☐ ....
☐ ....

Expenses: Investing/ Saving:

Item	Amount	Item	Amount

DAILY TRACKER

Date ....

Intention: ....

Affirmation: ....

Word of the Day: ....

7 :00	
:30	
8 :00	
:30	
9 :00	
:30	
10 :00	
:30	
11 :00	
:30	
12 :00	
:30	
1 :00	
:30	
2 :00	
:30	
3 :00	
:30	
4 :00	
:30	
5 :00	
:30	
6 :00	
:30	
7 :00	
:30	
8 :00	
:30	
9 :00	
:30	
10 :00	
:30	

- Exercise/Stretches: .... mins
- Pray/Meditation: .... mins
- Read/Audio: .... mins

I am reading /listening to:

_____

I Am Grateful for:
- ....
- ....
- ....
- ....
- ....

☐ I read my Monthly Declarations

To-Do's:
- ☐ ....
- ☐ ....
- ☐ ....
- ☐ ....
- ☐ ....

People to Contact:
- ☐ ....
- ☐ ....
- ☐ ....
- ☐ ....
- ☐ ....

Expenses: Investing/ Saving:

Item	Amount	Item	Amount

DAILY TRACKER

Date_____

Intention:_____

Affirmation:_____

Word of the Day:_____

7 :00	_____
:30	_____
8 :00	_____
:30	_____
9 :00	_____
:30	_____
10 :00	_____
:30	_____
11 :00	_____
:30	_____
12 :00	_____
:30	_____
1 :00	_____
:30	_____
2 :00	_____
:30	_____
3 :00	_____
:30	_____
4 :00	_____
:30	_____
5 :00	_____
:30	_____
6 :00	_____
:30	_____
7 :00	_____
:30	_____
8 :00	_____
:30	_____
9 :00	_____
:30	_____
10 :00	_____
:30	_____

- Exercise/Stretches: _____ mins
- Pray/Meditation: _____ mins
- Read/Audio: _____ mins

I am reading /listening to:

_____

I Am Grateful for:

- _____
- _____
- _____
- _____
- _____

☐ I read my Monthly Declarations

To-Do's:

☐ _____
☐ _____
☐ _____
☐ _____
☐ _____

People to Contact:

☐ _____
☐ _____
☐ _____
☐ _____
☐ _____

Expenses: Investing/ Saving:

Item	Amount	Item	Amount

DAILY TRACKER

Date ....

Intention: ....

Affirmation: ....

Word of the Day: ....

7 :00	
:30	
8 :00	
:30	
9 :00	
:30	
10 :00	
:30	
11 :00	
:30	
12 :00	
:30	
1 :00	
:30	
2 :00	
:30	
3 :00	
:30	
4 :00	
:30	
5 :00	
:30	
6 :00	
:30	
7 :00	
:30	
8 :00	
:30	
9 :00	
:30	
10 :00	
:30	

- Exercise/Stretches: .... mins
- Pray/Meditation: .... mins
- Read/Audio: .... mins

I am reading /listening to:

_____

I Am Grateful for:

- ....
- ....
- ....
- ....
- ....

☐ I read my Monthly Declarations

To-Do's:

☐ ....
☐ ....
☐ ....
☐ ....
☐ ....

People to Contact:

☐ ....
☐ ....
☐ ....
☐ ....
☐ ....

Expenses: Investing/ Saving:

Item	Amount	Item	Amount

DAILY TRACKER

Date _____

Intention: _____

Affirmation: _____

Word of the Day: _____

7 :00	
:30	
8 :00	
:30	
9 :00	
:30	
10 :00	
:30	
11 :00	
:30	
12 :00	
:30	
1 :00	
:30	
2 :00	
:30	
3 :00	
:30	
4 :00	
:30	
5 :00	
:30	
6 :00	
:30	
7 :00	
:30	
8 :00	
:30	
9 :00	
:30	
10 :00	
:30	

- Exercise/Stretches: _____ mins
- Pray/Meditation: _____ mins
- Read/Audio: _____ mins

I am reading /listening to:

_____

I Am Grateful for:
- _____
- _____
- _____
- _____
- _____

☐ I read my Monthly Declarations

To-Do's:
- ☐ _____
- ☐ _____
- ☐ _____
- ☐ _____
- ☐ _____

People to Contact:
- ☐ _____
- ☐ _____
- ☐ _____
- ☐ _____
- ☐ _____

Expenses: Investing/ Saving:

Item	Amount	Item	Amount

DAILY TRACKER

Date ....

Intention: ....

Affirmation: ....

Word of the Day: ....

7 :00	
:30	
8 :00	
:30	
9 :00	
:30	
10 :00	
:30	
11 :00	
:30	
12 :00	
:30	
1 :00	
:30	
2 :00	
:30	
3 :00	
:30	
4 :00	
:30	
5 :00	
:30	
6 :00	
:30	
7 :00	
:30	
8 :00	
:30	
9 :00	
:30	
10 :00	
:30	

• Exercise/Stretches: .... mins

• Pray/Meditation: .... mins

• Read/Audio: .... mins

I am reading /listening to:

_____

I Am Grateful for:

• ....

• ....

• ....

• ....

• ....

☐ I read my Monthly Declarations

To-Do's:

☐ ....

☐ ....

☐ ....

☐ ....

☐ ....

People to Contact:

☐ ....

☐ ....

☐ ....

☐ ....

☐ ....

Expenses: Investing/ Saving:

Item	Amount	Item	Amount

⚘ DAILY TRACKER ⚘

Date ....

Intention: ....
....
Affirmation: ....
Word of the Day: ....

7 :00	
:30	
8 :00	
:30	
9 :00	
:30	
10 :00	
:30	
11 :00	
:30	
12 :00	
:30	
1 :00	
:30	
2 :00	
:30	
3 :00	
:30	
4 :00	
:30	
5 :00	
:30	
6 :00	
:30	
7 :00	
:30	
8 :00	
:30	
9 :00	
:30	
10 :00	
:30	

- Exercise/Stretches: .... mins
- Pray/Meditation: .... mins
- Read/Audio: .... mins

I am reading /listening to:

_____

I Am Grateful for:
- ....
- ....
- ....
- ....
- ....

☐ I read my Monthly Declarations

To-Do's:
☐ ....
☐ ....
☐ ....
☐ ....
☐ ....

People to Contact:
☐ ....
☐ ....
☐ ....
☐ ....
☐ ....

Expenses: Investing/ Saving:

Item	Amount	Item	Amount

DAILY TRACKER

Date ....

Intention: ....

Affirmation: ....

Word of the Day: ....

7 :00	
:30	
8 :00	
:30	
9 :00	
:30	
10 :00	
:30	
11 :00	
:30	
12 :00	
:30	
1 :00	
:30	
2 :00	
:30	
3 :00	
:30	
4 :00	
:30	
5 :00	
:30	
6 :00	
:30	
7 :00	
:30	
8 :00	
:30	
9 :00	
:30	
10 :00	
:30	

• Exercise/Stretches: .... mins
• Pray/Meditation: .... mins
• Read/Audio: .... mins

I am reading /listening to:

_____

I Am Grateful for:
• ....
• ....
• ....
• ....
• ....

☐ I read my Monthly Declarations

To-Do's:
☐ ....
☐ ....
☐ ....
☐ ....
☐ ....

People to Contact:
☐ ....
☐ ....
☐ ....
☐ ....
☐

Expenses: Investing/ Saving:

Item	Amount	Item	Amount

DAILY TRACKER

Date ....

Intention: ....

Affirmation: ....

Word of the Day: ....

7 :00	
:30	
8 :00	
:30	
9 :00	
:30	
10 :00	
:30	
11 :00	
:30	
12 :00	
:30	
1 :00	
:30	
2 :00	
:30	
3 :00	
:30	
4 :00	
:30	
5 :00	
:30	
6 :00	
:30	
7 :00	
:30	
8 :00	
:30	
9 :00	
:30	
10 :00	
:30	

- Exercise/Stretches: .... mins
- Pray/Meditation: .... mins
- Read/Audio: .... mins

I am reading /listening to:

_____

I Am Grateful for:

- ....
- ....
- ....
- ....
- ....

☐ I read my Monthly Declarations

To-Do's:

☐ ....
☐ ....
☐ ....
☐ ....
☐ ....

People to Contact:

☐ ....
☐ ....
☐ ....
☐ ....
☐ ....

Expenses: Investing/ Saving:

Item	Amount	Item	Amount

DAILY TRACKER

Date ....

Intention: ....
Affirmation: ....
Word of the Day: ....

7 :00	_____
:30	_____
8 :00	_____
:30	_____
9 :00	_____
:30	_____
10 :00	_____
:30	_____
11 :00	_____
:30	_____
12 :00	_____
:30	_____
1 :00	_____
:30	_____
2 :00	_____
:30	_____
3 :00	_____
:30	_____
4 :00	_____
:30	_____
5 :00	_____
:30	_____
6 :00	_____
:30	_____
7 :00	_____
:30	_____
8 :00	_____
:30	_____
9 :00	_____
:30	_____
10 :00	_____
:30	_____

- Exercise/Stretches: .... mins
- Pray/Meditation: .... mins
- Read/Audio: .... mins

I am reading /listening to:

_____

I Am Grateful for:

- ....
- ....
- ....
- ....
- ....

☐ I read my Monthly Declarations

To-Do's:
☐ ....
☐ ....
☐ ....
☐ ....
☐ ....

People to Contact:
☐ ....
☐ ....
☐ ....
☐ ....
☐ ....

Expenses: Investing/ Saving:

Item	Amount	Item	Amount

DAILY TRACKER

Date ....

Intention: ....
Affirmation: ....
Word of the Day: ....

7 :00	
:30	
8 :00	
:30	
9 :00	
:30	
10 :00	
:30	
11 :00	
:30	
12 :00	
:30	
1 :00	
:30	
2 :00	
:30	
3 :00	
:30	
4 :00	
:30	
5 :00	
:30	
6 :00	
:30	
7 :00	
:30	
8 :00	
:30	
9 :00	
:30	
10 :00	
:30	

- Exercise/Stretches: .... mins
- Pray/Meditation: .... mins
- Read/Audio: .... mins

I am reading /listening to:

_____

I Am Grateful for:
- ....
- ....
- ....
- ....
- ....

☐ I read my Monthly Declarations

To-Do's:
- ☐ ....
- ☐ ....
- ☐ ....
- ☐ ....
- ☐ ....

People to Contact:
- ☐ ....
- ☐ ....
- ☐ ....
- ☐ ....
- ☐ ....

Expenses: Investing/ Saving:

Item	Amount	Item	Amount

DAILY TRACKER

Date ....

Intention: ....

Affirmation: ....

Word of the Day: ....

7 :00	
:30	
8 :00	
:30	
9 :00	
:30	
10 :00	
:30	
11 :00	
:30	
12 :00	
:30	
1 :00	
:30	
2 :00	
:30	
3 :00	
:30	
4 :00	
:30	
5 :00	
:30	
6 :00	
:30	
7 :00	
:30	
8 :00	
:30	
9 :00	
:30	
10 :00	
:30	

- Exercise/Stretches: .... mins
- Pray/Meditation: .... mins
- Read/Audio: .... mins

I am reading /listening to:

_____

I Am Grateful for:

- ....
- ....
- ....
- ....
- ....

☐ I read my Monthly Declarations

To-Do's:

☐ ....
☐ ....
☐ ....
☐ ....
☐ ....

People to Contact:

☐ ....
☐ ....
☐ ....
☐ ....
☐ ....

Expenses: Investing/ Saving:

Item	Amount	Item	Amount

DAILY TRACKER

Date _____

Intention: _____

Affirmation: _____

Word of the Day: _____

7 :00	
:30	
8 :00	
:30	
9 :00	
:30	
10 :00	
:30	
11 :00	
:30	
12 :00	
:30	
1 :00	
:30	
2 :00	
:30	
3 :00	
:30	
4 :00	
:30	
5 :00	
:30	
6 :00	
:30	
7 :00	
:30	
8 :00	
:30	
9 :00	
:30	
10 :00	
:30	

- Exercise/Stretches: _____ mins
- Pray/Meditation: _____ mins
- Read/Audio: _____ mins

I am reading /listening to:

_____

I Am Grateful for:
- _____
- _____
- _____
- _____
- _____

☐ I read my Monthly Declarations

To-Do's:
☐ _____
☐ _____
☐ _____
☐ _____
☐ _____

People to Contact:
☐ _____
☐ _____
☐ _____
☐ _____
☐ _____

Expenses: Investing/ Saving:

Item	Amount	Item	Amount

❧ DAILY TRACKER ❧

Date ....

Intention: ....

Affirmation: ....

Word of the Day: ....

7 :00	
:30	
8 :00	
:30	
9 :00	
:30	
10 :00	
:30	
11 :00	
:30	
12 :00	
:30	
1 :00	
:30	
2 :00	
:30	
3 :00	
:30	
4 :00	
:30	
5 :00	
:30	
6 :00	
:30	
7 :00	
:30	
8 :00	
:30	
9 :00	
:30	
10 :00	
:30	

- Exercise/Stretches: .... mins
- Pray/Meditation: .... mins
- Read/Audio: .... mins

I am reading /listening to:

_____

I Am Grateful for:

- • ....
- • ....
- • ....
- • ....
- • ....

☐ I read my Monthly Declarations

To-Do's:

☐ ....
☐ ....
☐ ....
☐ ....
☐ ....

People to Contact:

☐ ....
☐ ....
☐ ....
☐ ....
☐ ....

Expenses: Investing/ Saving:

Item	Amount	Item	Amount

DAILY TRACKER

Date ....

Intention: ....
Affirmation: ....
Word of the Day: ....

7 :00		
:30		
8 :00		
:30		
9 :00		
:30		
10 :00		
:30		
11 :00		
:30		
12 :00		
:30		
1 :00		
:30		
2 :00		
:30		
3 :00		
:30		
4 :00		
:30		
5 :00		
:30		
6 :00		
:30		
7 :00		
:30		
8 :00		
:30		
9 :00		
:30		
10 :00		
:30		

• Exercise/Stretches: .... mins
• Pray/Meditation: .... mins
• Read/Audio: .... mins

I am reading /listening to:

_____

I Am Grateful for:

- • ....
- • ....
- • ....
- • ....
- • ....

☐ I read my Monthly Declarations

To-Do's:

☐ ....
☐ ....
☐ ....
☐ ....
☐ ....

People to Contact:

☐ ....
☐ ....
☐ ....
☐ ....
☐ ....

Expenses: Investing/ Saving:

Item	Amount	Item	Amount

DAILY TRACKER

Date ....

Intention: ....

Affirmation: ....

Word of the Day: ....

7 :00	
:30	
8 :00	
:30	
9 :00	
:30	
10 :00	
:30	
11 :00	
:30	
12 :00	
:30	
1 :00	
:30	
2 :00	
:30	
3 :00	
:30	
4 :00	
:30	
5 :00	
:30	
6 :00	
:30	
7 :00	
:30	
8 :00	
:30	
9 :00	
:30	
10 :00	
:30	

- Exercise/Stretches: .... mins
- Pray/Meditation: .... mins
- Read/Audio: .... mins

I am reading /listening to:

_____

I Am Grateful for:

- ....
- ....
- ....
- ....
- ....

☐ I read my Monthly Declarations

To-Do's:

☐ ....
☐ ....
☐ ....
☐ ....
☐ ....

People to Contact:

☐ ....
☐ ....
☐ ....
☐ ....
☐ ....

Expenses: Investing/ Saving:

Item	Amount	Item	Amount

DAILY TRACKER

Date ....

Intention: ....
Affirmation: ....
Word of the Day: ....

7 :00	
:30	
8 :00	
:30	
9 :00	
:30	
10 :00	
:30	
11 :00	
:30	
12 :00	
:30	
1 :00	
:30	
2 :00	
:30	
3 :00	
:30	
4 :00	
:30	
5 :00	
:30	
6 :00	
:30	
7 :00	
:30	
8 :00	
:30	
9 :00	
:30	
10 :00	
:30	

- Exercise/Stretches: .... mins
- Pray/Meditation: .... mins
- Read/Audio: .... mins

I am reading /listening to:

_____

I Am Grateful for:

- ....
- ....
- ....
- ....
- ....

☐ I read my Monthly Declarations

To-Do's:

☐ ....
☐ ....
☐ ....
☐ ....
☐ ....

People to Contact:

☐ ....
☐ ....
☐ ....
☐ ....
☐ ....

Expenses: Investing/ Saving:

Item	Amount	Item	Amount

❧ DAILY TRACKER ❧

Date ....

Intention: ....
Affirmation: ....
Word of the Day: ....

7 :00	
:30	
8 :00	
:30	
9 :00	
:30	
10 :00	
:30	
11 :00	
:30	
12 :00	
:30	
1 :00	
:30	
2 :00	
:30	
3 :00	
:30	
4 :00	
:30	
5 :00	
:30	
6 :00	
:30	
7 :00	
:30	
8 :00	
:30	
9 :00	
:30	
10 :00	
:30	

- Exercise/Stretches: .... mins
- Pray/Meditation: .... mins
- Read/Audio: .... mins

I am reading /listening to:

_____

I Am Grateful for:
- ....
- ....
- ....
- ....
- ....

☐ I read my Monthly Declarations

To-Do's:
☐ ....
☐ ....
☐ ....
☐ ....
☐ ....

People to Contact:
☐ ....
☐ ....
☐ ....
☐ ....
☐ ....

Expenses: Investing/ Saving:

Item	Amount	Item	Amount

DAILY TRACKER

Date_____

Intention:_____
_____
Affirmation:_____
Word of the Day: _____

7 :00	
:30	
8 :00	
:30	
9 :00	
:30	
10 :00	
:30	
11 :00	
:30	
12 :00	
:30	
1 :00	
:30	
2 :00	
:30	
3 :00	
:30	
4 :00	
:30	
5 :00	
:30	
6 :00	
:30	
7 :00	
:30	
8 :00	
:30	
9 :00	
:30	
10 :00	
:30	

- Exercise/Stretches: _____ mins
- Pray/Meditation: _____ mins
- Read/Audio: _____ mins

I am reading /listening to:

_____

I Am Grateful for:
- _____
- _____
- _____
- _____
- _____

☐ I read my Monthly Declarations

To-Do's:
- ☐ _____
- ☐ _____
- ☐ _____
- ☐ _____
- ☐ _____

People to Contact:
- ☐ _____
- ☐ _____
- ☐ _____
- ☐ _____
- ☐ _____

Expenses: Investing/ Saving:

Item	Amount	Item	Amount

DAILY TRACKER

Date_____

Intention:_____

Affirmation:_____

Word of the Day: _____

7 :00	
:30	
8 :00	
:30	
9 :00	
:30	
10 :00	
:30	
11 :00	
:30	
12 :00	
:30	
1 :00	
:30	
2 :00	
:30	
3 :00	
:30	
4 :00	
:30	
5 :00	
:30	
6 :00	
:30	
7 :00	
:30	
8 :00	
:30	
9 :00	
:30	
10 :00	
:30	

• Exercise/Stretches: _____ mins
• Pray/Meditation: _____ mins
• Read/Audio: _____ mins

I am reading /listening to:

_____

I Am Grateful for:

• _____
• _____
• _____
• _____
• _____

☐ I read my Monthly Declarations

To-Do's:
☐ _____
☐ _____
☐ _____
☐ _____
☐ _____

People to Contact:
☐ _____
☐ _____
☐ _____
☐ _____
☐ _____

Expenses: Investing/ Saving:

Item	Amount	Item	Amount

DAILY TRACKER

Date................................

Intention:...
Affirmation:..
Word of the Day: ....

7	:00	_____
	:30	_____
8	:00	_____
	:30	_____
9	:00	_____
	:30	_____
10	:00	_____
	:30	_____
11	:00	_____
	:30	_____
12	:00	_____
	:30	_____
1	:00	_____
	:30	_____
2	:00	_____
	:30	_____
3	:00	_____
	:30	_____
4	:00	_____
	:30	_____
5	:00	_____
	:30	_____
6	:00	_____
	:30	_____
7	:00	_____
	:30	_____
8	:00	_____
	:30	_____
9	:00	_____
	:30	_____
10	:00	_____
	:30	_____

- Exercise/Stretches: .... mins
- Pray/Meditation: .... mins
- Read/Audio: .... mins

I am reading /listening to:

_____

I Am Grateful for:

- ....
- ....
- ....
- ....
- ....

☐ I read my Monthly Declarations

To-Do's:

☐ ....
☐ ....
☐ ....
☐ ....
☐ ....

People to Contact:

☐ ....
☐ ....
☐ ....
☐ ....
☐ ....

Expenses: Investing/ Saving:

Item	Amount	Item	Amount

❧ DAILY TRACKER ☙

Date ....

Intention: ....
Affirmation: ....
Word of the Day: ....

7 :00	
:30	
8 :00	
:30	
9 :00	
:30	
10 :00	
:30	
11 :00	
:30	
12 :00	
:30	
1 :00	
:30	
2 :00	
:30	
3 :00	
:30	
4 :00	
:30	
5 :00	
:30	
6 :00	
:30	
7 :00	
:30	
8 :00	
:30	
9 :00	
:30	
10 :00	
:30	

- Exercise/Stretches: .... mins
- Pray/Meditation: .... mins
- Read/Audio: .... mins

I am reading /listening to:
_____

I Am Grateful for:
- ....
- ....
- ....
- ....
- ....

☐ I read my Monthly Declarations

To-Do's:
☐ ....
☐ ....
☐ ....
☐ ....
☐ ....

People to Contact:
☐ ....
☐ ....
☐ ....
☐ ....
☐ ....

Expenses: Investing/ Saving:

Item	Amount	Item	Amount

❧ DAILY TRACKER ❦

Date _____

Intention: _____
_____
Affirmation: _____
Word of the Day: _____

7 :00	
:30	
8 :00	
:30	
9 :00	
:30	
10 :00	
:30	
11 :00	
:30	
12 :00	
:30	
1 :00	
:30	
2 :00	
:30	
3 :00	
:30	
4 :00	
:30	
5 :00	
:30	
6 :00	
:30	
7 :00	
:30	
8 :00	
:30	
9 :00	
:30	
10 :00	
:30	

- Exercise/Stretches: _____ mins
- Pray/Meditation: _____ mins
- Read/Audio: _____ mins

I am reading /listening to:

_____

I Am Grateful for:

- _____
- _____
- _____
- _____
- _____

☐ I read my Monthly Declarations

To-Do's:

☐ _____
☐ _____
☐ _____
☐ _____
☐ _____

People to Contact:

☐ _____
☐ _____
☐ _____
☐ _____
☐ _____

Expenses: Investing/ Saving:

Item	Amount	Item	Amount

✿ DAILY TRACKER ✿

Date ....

Intention: ....
Affirmation: ....
Word of the Day: ....

7 :00	
:30	
8 :00	
:30	
9 :00	
:30	
10 :00	
:30	
11 :00	
:30	
12 :00	
:30	
1 :00	
:30	
2 :00	
:30	
3 :00	
:30	
4 :00	
:30	
5 :00	
:30	
6 :00	
:30	
7 :00	
:30	
8 :00	
:30	
9 :00	
:30	
10 :00	
:30	

- Exercise/Stretches: .... mins
- Pray/Meditation: .... mins
- Read/Audio: .... mins

I am reading /listening to:

_____

I Am Grateful for:
- ....
- ....
- ....
- ....
- ....

☐ I read my Monthly Declarations

To-Do's:
☐ ....
☐ ....
☐ ....
☐ ....
☐ ....

People to Contact:
☐ ....
☐ ....
☐ ....
☐ ....
☐ ....

Expenses: Investing/ Saving:

Item	Amount	Item	Amount

DAILY TRACKER

Date ....

Intention: ....
Affirmation: ....
Word of the Day: ....

7 :00	
:30	
8 :00	
:30	
9 :00	
:30	
10 :00	
:30	
11 :00	
:30	
12 :00	
:30	
1 :00	
:30	
2 :00	
:30	
3 :00	
:30	
4 :00	
:30	
5 :00	
:30	
6 :00	
:30	
7 :00	
:30	
8 :00	
:30	
9 :00	
:30	
10 :00	
:30	

- Exercise/Stretches: .... mins
- Pray/Meditation: .... mins
- Read/Audio: .... mins

I am reading /listening to:

_____

I Am Grateful for:
- ....
- ....
- ....
- ....
- ....

☐ I read my Monthly Declarations

To-Do's:
- ☐ ....
- ☐ ....
- ☐ ....
- ☐ ....
- ☐ ....

People to Contact:
- ☐ ....
- ☐ ....
- ☐ ....
- ☐ ....
- ☐ ....

Expenses: Investing/ Saving:

Item	Amount	Item	Amount

MONTHLY CHECK-IN

In this section spend quiet time reflecting on your month, what you created, what are some lessons learned, and in what ways are you committed to creating something different.

What's working:

_____
_____
_____
_____
_____
_____
_____
_____
_____
_____
_____

What's not working:

_____
_____
_____
_____
_____
_____
_____
_____
_____

What am I committed to doing differently to create different results?

_____
_____
_____
_____
_____
_____
_____
_____
_____
_____

Month

MONTHLY EXPENSE TRACKER

Date	Expense Category	Budget	Actual
	Donating/Tithing		
	Living Expenses		
	Rent/ Mortgage		
Total		$	$

MONTHLY INCOME & SAVINGS TRACKER

Date	Income	Savings/ Investing	Account
Total	$	$	

MONTHLY NOTES / JOURNAL

MONTHLY DECLARATIONS

What do you want to achieve in all areas of your life this month?

Faith/Spirituality:

- _____
- _____
- _____

Mindset/Personal   Development:

- _____
- _____
- _____

Family/Relationships:

- _____
- _____
- _____

Health/Fitness:

- _____
- _____
- _____

Business/Career:

- _____
- _____
- _____

Community/Contribution:

- _____
- _____
- _____

Money/Finances:

- _____
- _____
- _____

I, (full name) _____

declare to accomplish the above handwritten goals in excellence by (date) _____

DAILY TRACKER

Date ....

Intention: ....
Affirmation: ....
Word of the Day: ....

7 :00	
:30	
8 :00	
:30	
9 :00	
:30	
10 :00	
:30	
11 :00	
:30	
12 :00	
:30	
1 :00	
:30	
2 :00	
:30	
3 :00	
:30	
4 :00	
:30	
5 :00	
:30	
6 :00	
:30	
7 :00	
:30	
8 :00	
:30	
9 :00	
:30	
10 :00	
:30	

- Exercise/Stretches: .... mins
- Pray/Meditation: .... mins
- Read/Audio: .... mins

I am reading /listening to:

_____

I Am Grateful for:

- ....
- ....
- ....
- ....
- ....

☐ I read my Monthly Declarations

To-Do's:

☐ ....
☐ ....
☐ ....
☐ ....
☐ ....

People to Contact:

☐ ....
☐ ....
☐ ....
☐ ....
☐ ....

Expenses: Investing/ Saving:

Item	Amount	Item	Amount

DAILY TRACKER

Date ....

Intention: ....
Affirmation: ....
Word of the Day: ....

7 :00		
:30		
8 :00		
:30		
9 :00		
:30		
10 :00		
:30		
11 :00		
:30		
12 :00		
:30		
1 :00		
:30		
2 :00		
:30		
3 :00		
:30		
4 :00		
:30		
5 :00		
:30		
6 :00		
:30		
7 :00		
:30		
8 :00		
:30		
9 :00		
:30		
10 :00		
:30		

- Exercise/Stretches: .... mins
- Pray/Meditation: .... mins
- Read/Audio: .... mins

I am reading /listening to:

_____

I Am Grateful for:
- ....
- ....
- ....
- ....
- ....

☐ I read my Monthly Declarations

To-Do's:
☐ ....
☐ ....
☐ ....
☐ ....
☐ ....

People to Contact:
☐ ....
☐ ....
☐ ....
☐ ....
☐ ....

Expenses: Investing/ Saving:

Item	Amount	Item	Amount

DAILY TRACKER

Date _____

Intention: _____

Affirmation: _____

Word of the Day: _____

7 :00		
:30		
8 :00		
:30		
9 :00		
:30		
10 :00		
:30		
11 :00		
:30		
12 :00		
:30		
1 :00		
:30		
2 :00		
:30		
3 :00		
:30		
4 :00		
:30		
5 :00		
:30		
6 :00		
:30		
7 :00		
:30		
8 :00		
:30		
9 :00		
:30		
10 :00		
:30		

- Exercise/Stretches: .... mins
- Pray/Meditation: .... mins
- Read/Audio: .... mins

I am reading /listening to:

_____

I Am Grateful for:

- _____
- _____
- _____
- _____
- _____

☐ I read my Monthly Declarations

To-Do's:

☐ _____
☐ _____
☐ _____
☐ _____
☐ _____

People to Contact:

☐ _____
☐ _____
☐ _____
☐ _____
☐ _____

Expenses: Investing/ Saving:

Item	Amount	Item	Amount

DAILY TRACKER

Date ....

Intention: ....

Affirmation: ....

Word of the Day: ....

7 :00	
:30	
8 :00	
:30	
9 :00	
:30	
10 :00	
:30	
11 :00	
:30	
12 :00	
:30	
1 :00	
:30	
2 :00	
:30	
3 :00	
:30	
4 :00	
:30	
5 :00	
:30	
6 :00	
:30	
7 :00	
:30	
8 :00	
:30	
9 :00	
:30	
10 :00	
:30	

- Exercise/Stretches: .... mins
- Pray/Meditation: .... mins
- Read/Audio: .... mins

I am reading /listening to:

_____

I Am Grateful for:

- ....
- ....
- ....
- ....
- ....

☐ I read my Monthly Declarations

To-Do's:

☐ ....
☐ ....
☐ ....
☐ ....
☐ ....

People to Contact:

☐ ....
☐ ....
☐ ....
☐ ....
☐ ....

Expenses: Investing/ Saving:

Item	Amount	Item	Amount

DAILY TRACKER

Date ....

Intention: ....

Affirmation: ....

Word of the Day: ....

7 :00	
:30	
8 :00	
:30	
9 :00	
:30	
10 :00	
:30	
11 :00	
:30	
12 :00	
:30	
1 :00	
:30	
2 :00	
:30	
3 :00	
:30	
4 :00	
:30	
5 :00	
:30	
6 :00	
:30	
7 :00	
:30	
8 :00	
:30	
9 :00	
:30	
10 :00	
:30	

- Exercise/Stretches: .... mins
- Pray/Meditation: .... mins
- Read/Audio: .... mins

I am reading /listening to:

_____

I Am Grateful for:

- ....
- ....
- ....
- ....
- ....

☐ I read my Monthly Declarations

To-Do's:

☐ ....
☐ ....
☐ ....
☐ ....
☐ ....

People to Contact:

☐ ....
☐ ....
☐ ....
☐ ....
☐ ....

Expenses: Investing/ Saving:

Item	Amount	Item	Amount

DAILY TRACKER

Date ....

Intention: ....
Affirmation: ....
Word of the Day: ....

7 :00	
:30	
8 :00	
:30	
9 :00	
:30	
10 :00	
:30	
11 :00	
:30	
12 :00	
:30	
1 :00	
:30	
2 :00	
:30	
3 :00	
:30	
4 :00	
:30	
5 :00	
:30	
6 :00	
:30	
7 :00	
:30	
8 :00	
:30	
9 :00	
:30	
10 :00	
:30	

- Exercise/Stretches: .... mins
- Pray/Meditation: .... mins
- Read/Audio: .... mins

I am reading /listening to:

_____

I Am Grateful for:

- ....
- ....
- ....
- ....
- ....

☐ I read my Monthly Declarations

To-Do's:
☐ ....
☐ ....
☐ ....
☐ ....
☐ ....

People to Contact:
☐ ....
☐ ....
☐ ....
☐ ....
☐ ....

Expenses: Investing/ Saving:

Item	Amount	Item	Amount

DAILY TRACKER

Date _____

Intention: _____

Affirmation: _____

Word of the Day: _____

7 :00	
:30	
8 :00	
:30	
9 :00	
:30	
10 :00	
:30	
11 :00	
:30	
12 :00	
:30	
1 :00	
:30	
2 :00	
:30	
3 :00	
:30	
4 :00	
:30	
5 :00	
:30	
6 :00	
:30	
7 :00	
:30	
8 :00	
:30	
9 :00	
:30	
10 :00	
:30	

- Exercise/Stretches: .... mins
- Pray/Meditation: .... mins
- Read/Audio: .... mins

I am reading /listening to:

_____

I Am Grateful for:

- ....
- ....
- ....
- ....
- ....

☐ I read my Monthly Declarations

To-Do's:
☐ ....
☐ ....
☐ ....
☐ ....
☐ ....

People to Contact:
☐ ....
☐ ....
☐ ....
☐ ....
☐ ....

Expenses: Investing/ Saving:

Item	Amount	Item	Amount

DAILY TRACKER

Date ....

Intention: ....
....
Affirmation: ....
Word of the Day: ....

7	:00	
	:30	
8	:00	
	:30	
9	:00	
	:30	
10	:00	
	:30	
11	:00	
	:30	
12	:00	
	:30	
1	:00	
	:30	
2	:00	
	:30	
3	:00	
	:30	
4	:00	
	:30	
5	:00	
	:30	
6	:00	
	:30	
7	:00	
	:30	
8	:00	
	:30	
9	:00	
	:30	
10	:00	
	:30	

- Exercise/Stretches: .... mins
- Pray/Meditation: .... mins
- Read/Audio: .... mins

I am reading /listening to:

_____

I Am Grateful for:

- ....
- ....
- ....
- ....
- ....

☐ I read my Monthly Declarations

To-Do's:

☐ ....
☐ ....
☐ ....
☐ ....
☐ ....

People to Contact:

☐ ....
☐ ....
☐ ....
☐ ....
☐ ....

Expenses: Investing/ Saving:

Item	Amount	Item	Amount

DAILY TRACKER

Date_____

Intention:_____

Affirmation:_____

Word of the Day: _____

7 :00	_____
:30	_____
8 :00	_____
:30	_____
9 :00	_____
:30	_____
10 :00	_____
:30	_____
11 :00	_____
:30	_____
12 :00	_____
:30	_____
1 :00	_____
:30	_____
2 :00	_____
:30	_____
3 :00	_____
:30	_____
4 :00	_____
:30	_____
5 :00	_____
:30	_____
6 :00	_____
:30	_____
7 :00	_____
:30	_____
8 :00	_____
:30	_____
9 :00	_____
:30	_____
10 :00	_____
:30	_____

- Exercise/Stretches: _____ mins
- Pray/Meditation: _____ mins
- Read/Audio: _____ mins

I am reading /listening to:

_____

I Am Grateful for:

- _____
- _____
- _____
- _____
- _____

☐ I read my Monthly Declarations

To-Do's:

☐ _____
☐ _____
☐ _____
☐ _____
☐ _____

People to Contact:

☐ _____
☐ _____
☐ _____
☐ _____
☐ _____

Expenses: Investing/ Saving:

Item	Amount	Item	Amount

DAILY TRACKER

Date ....

Intention: ....
....
Affirmation: ....
Word of the Day: ....

7	:00	
	:30	
8	:00	
	:30	
9	:00	
	:30	
10	:00	
	:30	
11	:00	
	:30	
12	:00	
	:30	
1	:00	
	:30	
2	:00	
	:30	
3	:00	
	:30	
4	:00	
	:30	
5	:00	
	:30	
6	:00	
	:30	
7	:00	
	:30	
8	:00	
	:30	
9	:00	
	:30	
10	:00	
	:30	

• Exercise/Stretches: .... mins
• Pray/Meditation: .... mins
• Read/Audio: .... mins

I am reading /listening to:

_____

I Am Grateful for:
• ....
• ....
• ....
• ....
• ....

☐ I read my Monthly Declarations

To-Do's:
☐ ....
☐ ....
☐ ....
☐ ....
☐ ....

People to Contact:
☐ ....
☐ ....
☐ ....
☐ ....
☐ ....

Expenses: Investing/ Saving:

Item	Amount	Item	Amount

DAILY TRACKER

Date ....

Intention: ....

Affirmation: ....

Word of the Day: ....

7 :00	
:30	
8 :00	
:30	
9 :00	
:30	
10 :00	
:30	
11 :00	
:30	
12 :00	
:30	
1 :00	
:30	
2 :00	
:30	
3 :00	
:30	
4 :00	
:30	
5 :00	
:30	
6 :00	
:30	
7 :00	
:30	
8 :00	
:30	
9 :00	
:30	
10 :00	
:30	

- Exercise/Stretches: .... mins
- Pray/Meditation: .... mins
- Read/Audio: .... mins

I am reading /listening to:

_____

I Am Grateful for:

- ....
- ....
- ....
- ....
- ....

☐ I read my Monthly Declarations

To-Do's:

☐ ....
☐ ....
☐ ....
☐ ....
☐ ....

People to Contact:

☐ ....
☐ ....
☐ ....
☐ ....
☐ ....

Expenses: Investing/ Saving:

Item	Amount	Item	Amount

DAILY TRACKER

Date ....

Intention: ....
Affirmation: ....
Word of the Day: ....

7 :00	
:30	
8 :00	
:30	
9 :00	
:30	
10 :00	
:30	
11 :00	
:30	
12 :00	
:30	
1 :00	
:30	
2 :00	
:30	
3 :00	
:30	
4 :00	
:30	
5 :00	
:30	
6 :00	
:30	
7 :00	
:30	
8 :00	
:30	
9 :00	
:30	
10 :00	
:30	

- Exercise/Stretches: .... mins
- Pray/Meditation: .... mins
- Read/Audio: .... mins

I am reading /listening to:

_____

I Am Grateful for:
- ....
- ....
- ....
- ....
- ....

☐ I read my Monthly Declarations

To-Do's:
☐ ....
☐ ....
☐ ....
☐ ....
☐ ....

People to Contact:
☐ ....
☐ ....
☐ ....
☐ ....
☐ ....

Expenses: Investing/ Saving:

Item	Amount	Item	Amount

DAILY TRACKER

Date ....

Intention: ....
Affirmation: ....
Word of the Day: ....

7 :00	
:30	
8 :00	
:30	
9 :00	
:30	
10 :00	
:30	
11 :00	
:30	
12 :00	
:30	
1 :00	
:30	
2 :00	
:30	
3 :00	
:30	
4 :00	
:30	
5 :00	
:30	
6 :00	
:30	
7 :00	
:30	
8 :00	
:30	
9 :00	
:30	
10 :00	
:30	

- Exercise/Stretches: .... mins
- Pray/Meditation: .... mins
- Read/Audio: .... mins

I am reading /listening to:

_____

I Am Grateful for:

- ....
- ....
- ....
- ....
- ....

☐ I read my Monthly Declarations

To-Do's:

☐ ....
☐ ....
☐ ....
☐ ....
☐ ....

People to Contact:

☐ ....
☐ ....
☐ ....
☐ ....
☐ ....

Expenses: Investing/ Saving:

Item	Amount	Item	Amount

⁙ *DAILY TRACKER* ⁙

Date ....

Intention: ....

Affirmation: ....

Word of the Day: ....

7 :00	
:30	
8 :00	
:30	
9 :00	
:30	
10 :00	
:30	
11 :00	
:30	
12 :00	
:30	
1 :00	
:30	
2 :00	
:30	
3 :00	
:30	
4 :00	
:30	
5 :00	
:30	
6 :00	
:30	
7 :00	
:30	
8 :00	
:30	
9 :00	
:30	
10 :00	
:30	

- Exercise/Stretches: .... mins
- Pray/Meditation: .... mins
- Read/Audio: .... mins

I am reading /listening to:

_____

I Am Grateful for:

- ....
- ....
- ....
- ....
- ....

☐ I read my Monthly Declarations

To-Do's:

☐ ....
☐ ....
☐ ....
☐ ....
☐ ....

People to Contact:

☐ ....
☐ ....
☐ ....
☐ ....
☐ ....

Expenses: Investing/ Saving:

Item	Amount	Item	Amount

❧ DAILY TRACKER ❧

Date_____

Intention:_____
Affirmation:_____
Word of the Day:_____

7 :00	
:30	
8 :00	
:30	
9 :00	
:30	
10 :00	
:30	
11 :00	
:30	
12 :00	
:30	
1 :00	
:30	
2 :00	
:30	
3 :00	
:30	
4 :00	
:30	
5 :00	
:30	
6 :00	
:30	
7 :00	
:30	
8 :00	
:30	
9 :00	
:30	
10 :00	
:30	

• Exercise/Stretches: _____ mins
• Pray/Meditation: _____ mins
• Read/Audio: _____ mins

I am reading /listening to:

_____

I Am Grateful for:

- • _____
- • _____
- • _____
- • _____
- • _____

☐ I read my Monthly Declarations

To-Do's:
- ☐ _____
- ☐ _____
- ☐ _____
- ☐ _____
- ☐ _____

People to Contact:
- ☐ _____
- ☐ _____
- ☐ _____
- ☐ _____
- ☐ _____

Expenses: Investing/ Saving:

Item	Amount	Item	Amount

⊱❧ DAILY TRACKER ☙⊰

Date ....

Intention: ....

Affirmation: ....

Word of the Day: ....

7 :00	
:30	
8 :00	
:30	
9 :00	
:30	
10 :00	
:30	
11 :00	
:30	
12 :00	
:30	
1 :00	
:30	
2 :00	
:30	
3 :00	
:30	
4 :00	
:30	
5 :00	
:30	
6 :00	
:30	
7 :00	
:30	
8 :00	
:30	
9 :00	
:30	
10 :00	
:30	

• Exercise/Stretches: .... mins
• Pray/Meditation: .... mins
• Read/Audio: .... mins

I am reading /listening to:

_____

I Am Grateful for:
• ....
• ....
• ....
• ....
• ....

☐ I read my Monthly Declarations

To-Do's:
☐ ....
☐ ....
☐ ....
☐ ....
☐ ....

People to Contact:
☐ ....
☐ ....
☐ ....
☐ ....
☐ ....

Expenses: Investing/ Saving:

Item	Amount	Item	Amount

DAILY TRACKER

Date ....

Intention: ....

Affirmation: ....

Word of the Day: ....

7 :00	
:30	
8 :00	
:30	
9 :00	
:30	
10 :00	
:30	
11 :00	
:30	
12 :00	
:30	
1 :00	
:30	
2 :00	
:30	
3 :00	
:30	
4 :00	
:30	
5 :00	
:30	
6 :00	
:30	
7 :00	
:30	
8 :00	
:30	
9 :00	
:30	
10 :00	
:30	

- Exercise/Stretches: .... mins
- Pray/Meditation: .... mins
- Read/Audio: .... mins

I am reading /listening to:

_____

I Am Grateful for:

- ....
- ....
- ....
- ....
- ....

☐ I read my Monthly Declarations

To-Do's:

☐ ....
☐ ....
☐ ....
☐ ....
☐ ....

People to Contact:

☐ ....
☐ ....
☐ ....
☐ ....
☐ ....

Expenses: Investing/ Saving:

Item	Amount	Item	Amount

DAILY TRACKER

Date ....

Intention: ....
....
Affirmation: ....
Word of the Day: ....

7 :00	
:30	
8 :00	
:30	
9 :00	
:30	
10 :00	
:30	
11 :00	
:30	
12 :00	
:30	
1 :00	
:30	
2 :00	
:30	
3 :00	
:30	
4 :00	
:30	
5 :00	
:30	
6 :00	
:30	
7 :00	
:30	
8 :00	
:30	
9 :00	
:30	
10 :00	
:30	

- Exercise/Stretches: .... mins
- Pray/Meditation: .... mins
- Read/Audio: .... mins

I am reading /listening to:

_____

I Am Grateful for:
- ....
- ....
- ....
- ....
- ....

☐ I read my Monthly Declarations

To-Do's:
☐ ....
☐ ....
☐ ....
☐ ....
☐ ....

People to Contact:
☐ ....
☐ ....
☐ ....
☐ ....
☐ ....

Expenses: Investing/ Saving:

Item	Amount	Item	Amount

DAILY TRACKER

Date ....

Intention: ....
Affirmation: ....
Word of the Day: ....

7 :00	
:30	
8 :00	
:30	
9 :00	
:30	
10 :00	
:30	
11 :00	
:30	
12 :00	
:30	
1 :00	
:30	
2 :00	
:30	
3 :00	
:30	
4 :00	
:30	
5 :00	
:30	
6 :00	
:30	
7 :00	
:30	
8 :00	
:30	
9 :00	
:30	
10 :00	
:30	

- Exercise/Stretches: .... mins
- Pray/Meditation: .... mins
- Read/Audio: .... mins

I am reading /listening to:

_____

I Am Grateful for:
- ....
- ....
- ....
- ....
- ....

☐ I read my Monthly Declarations

To-Do's:
☐ ....
☐ ....
☐ ....
☐ ....
☐

People to Contact:
☐ ....
☐ ....
☐ ....
☐ ....
☐ ....

Expenses: Investing/ Saving:

Item	Amount	Item	Amount

DAILY TRACKER

Date ....

Intention: ....
Affirmation: ....
Word of the Day: ....

7 :00	
:30	
8 :00	
:30	
9 :00	
:30	
10 :00	
:30	
11 :00	
:30	
12 :00	
:30	
1 :00	
:30	
2 :00	
:30	
3 :00	
:30	
4 :00	
:30	
5 :00	
:30	
6 :00	
:30	
7 :00	
:30	
8 :00	
:30	
9 :00	
:30	
10 :00	
:30	

- Exercise/Stretches: .... mins
- Pray/Meditation: .... mins
- Read/Audio: .... mins

I am reading /listening to:

_____

I Am Grateful for:
- ....
- ....
- ....
- ....
- ....

☐ I read my Monthly Declarations

To-Do's:
- ☐ ....
- ☐ ....
- ☐ ....
- ☐ ....
- ☐ ....

People to Contact:
- ☐ ....
- ☐ ....
- ☐ ....
- ☐ ....
- ☐ ....

Expenses: Investing/ Saving:

Item	Amount	Item	Amount

DAILY TRACKER

Date ....

Intention: ....
....
Affirmation: ....
Word of the Day: ....

7 :00	
:30	
8 :00	
:30	
9 :00	
:30	
10 :00	
:30	
11 :00	
:30	
12 :00	
:30	
1 :00	
:30	
2 :00	
:30	
3 :00	
:30	
4 :00	
:30	
5 :00	
:30	
6 :00	
:30	
7 :00	
:30	
8 :00	
:30	
9 :00	
:30	
10 :00	
:30	

- Exercise/Stretches: .... mins
- Pray/Meditation: .... mins
- Read/Audio: .... mins

I am reading /listening to:
_____

I Am Grateful for:
- ....
- ....
- ....
- ....
- ....

☐ I read my Monthly Declarations

To-Do's:
☐ ....
☐ ....
☐ ....
☐ ....
☐ ....

People to Contact:
☐ ....
☐ ....
☐ ....
☐ ....
☐ ....

Expenses: Investing/ Saving:

Item	Amount	Item	Amount

DAILY TRACKER

Date ....

Intention: ....

Affirmation: ....

Word of the Day: ....

7 :00	
:30	
8 :00	
:30	
9 :00	
:30	
10 :00	
:30	
11 :00	
:30	
12 :00	
:30	
1 :00	
:30	
2 :00	
:30	
3 :00	
:30	
4 :00	
:30	
5 :00	
:30	
6 :00	
:30	
7 :00	
:30	
8 :00	
:30	
9 :00	
:30	
10 :00	
:30	

- Exercise/Stretches: .... mins
- Pray/Meditation: .... mins
- Read/Audio: .... mins

I am reading /listening to:

_____

I Am Grateful for:
- ....
- ....
- ....
- ....
- ....

☐ I read my Monthly Declarations

To-Do's:
☐ ....
☐ ....
☐ ....
☐ ....
☐ ....

People to Contact:
☐ ....
☐ ....
☐ ....
☐ ....
☐ ....

Expenses: Investing/ Saving:

Item	Amount	Item	Amount

❧ DAILY TRACKER ❧

Date ....

Intention: ....
Affirmation: ....
Word of the Day: ....

7 :00	
:30	
8 :00	
:30	
9 :00	
:30	
10 :00	
:30	
11 :00	
:30	
12 :00	
:30	
1 :00	
:30	
2 :00	
:30	
3 :00	
:30	
4 :00	
:30	
5 :00	
:30	
6 :00	
:30	
7 :00	
:30	
8 :00	
:30	
9 :00	
:30	
10 :00	
:30	

• Exercise/Stretches: .... mins
• Pray/Meditation: .... mins
• Read/Audio: .... mins

I am reading /listening to:
_____

I Am Grateful for:
• ....
• ....
• ....
• ....
• ....

☐ I read my Monthly Declarations

To-Do's:
☐ ....
☐ ....
☐ ....
☐ ....
☐ ....

People to Contact:
☐ ....
☐ ....
☐ ....
☐ ....
☐ ....

Expenses: Investing/ Saving:

Item	Amount	Item	Amount

DAILY TRACKER

Date ....

Intention: ....

Affirmation: ....

Word of the Day: ....

7 :00	_____
:30	_____
8 :00	_____
:30	_____
9 :00	_____
:30	_____
10 :00	_____
:30	_____
11 :00	_____
:30	_____
12 :00	_____
:30	_____
1 :00	_____
:30	_____
2 :00	_____
:30	_____
3 :00	_____
:30	_____
4 :00	_____
:30	_____
5 :00	_____
:30	_____
6 :00	_____
:30	_____
7 :00	_____
:30	_____
8 :00	_____
:30	_____
9 :00	_____
:30	_____
10 :00	_____
:30	_____

- Exercise/Stretches: .... mins
- Pray/Meditation: .... mins
- Read/Audio: .... mins

I am reading /listening to:

_____

I Am Grateful for:

- ....
- ....
- ....
- ....
- ....

☐ I read my Monthly Declarations

To-Do's:

☐ ....
☐ ....
☐ ....
☐ ....
☐ ....

People to Contact:

☐ ....
☐ ....
☐ ....
☐ ....
☐ ....

Expenses: Investing/ Saving:

Item	Amount	Item	Amount

DAILY TRACKER

Date _____

Intention: _____
_____

Affirmation: _____

Word of the Day: _____

7 :00	
:30	
8 :00	
:30	
9 :00	
:30	
10 :00	
:30	
11 :00	
:30	
12 :00	
:30	
1 :00	
:30	
2 :00	
:30	
3 :00	
:30	
4 :00	
:30	
5 :00	
:30	
6 :00	
:30	
7 :00	
:30	
8 :00	
:30	
9 :00	
:30	
10 :00	
:30	

• Exercise/Stretches: _____ mins
• Pray/Meditation: _____ mins
• Read/Audio: _____ mins

I am reading /listening to:

_____

I Am Grateful for:

• _____
• _____
• _____
• _____
• _____

☐ I read my Monthly Declarations

To-Do's:

☐ _____
☐ _____
☐ _____
☐ _____
☐ _____

People to Contact:

☐ _____
☐ _____
☐ _____
☐ _____
☐ _____

Expenses: Investing/ Saving:

Item	Amount	Item	Amount

DAILY TRACKER

Date ....

Intention: ....
Affirmation: ....
Word of the Day: ....

7 :00	
:30	
8 :00	
:30	
9 :00	
:30	
10 :00	
:30	
11 :00	
:30	
12 :00	
:30	
1 :00	
:30	
2 :00	
:30	
3 :00	
:30	
4 :00	
:30	
5 :00	
:30	
6 :00	
:30	
7 :00	
:30	
8 :00	
:30	
9 :00	
:30	
10 :00	
:30	

- Exercise/Stretches: .... mins
- Pray/Meditation: .... mins
- Read/Audio: .... mins

I am reading /listening to:

_____

I Am Grateful for:
- ....
- ....
- ....
- ....
- ....

☐ I read my Monthly Declarations

To-Do's:
☐ ....
☐ ....
☐ ....
☐ ....
☐ ....

People to Contact:
☐ ....
☐ ....
☐ ....
☐ ....
☐ ....

Expenses: Investing/ Saving:

Item	Amount	Item	Amount

$\sim\!\!\!\!\diamond$ DAILY TRACKER $\diamond\!\!\!\!\sim$

Date_____

Intention:_____
Affirmation:_____
Word of the Day:_____

7 :00	
:30	
8 :00	
:30	
9 :00	
:30	
10 :00	
:30	
11 :00	
:30	
12 :00	
:30	
1 :00	
:30	
2 :00	
:30	
3 :00	
:30	
4 :00	
:30	
5 :00	
:30	
6 :00	
:30	
7 :00	
:30	
8 :00	
:30	
9 :00	
:30	
10 :00	
:30	

- Exercise/Stretches: _____ mins
- Pray/Meditation: _____ mins
- Read/Audio: _____ mins

I am reading /listening to:

_____

I Am Grateful for:

- _____
- _____
- _____
- _____
- _____

☐ I read my Monthly Declarations

To-Do's:

☐ _____
☐ _____
☐ _____
☐ _____
☐ _____

People to Contact:

☐ _____
☐ _____
☐ _____
☐ _____
☐ _____

Expenses: Investing/ Saving:

Item	Amount	Item	Amount

DAILY TRACKER

Date ....

Intention: ....

Affirmation: ....

Word of the Day: ....

7 :00	
:30	
8 :00	
:30	
9 :00	
:30	
10 :00	
:30	
11 :00	
:30	
12 :00	
:30	
1 :00	
:30	
2 :00	
:30	
3 :00	
:30	
4 :00	
:30	
5 :00	
:30	
6 :00	
:30	
7 :00	
:30	
8 :00	
:30	
9 :00	
:30	
10 :00	
:30	

- Exercise/Stretches: .... mins
- Pray/Meditation: .... mins
- Read/Audio: .... mins

I am reading /listening to:

_____

I Am Grateful for:

- ....
- ....
- ....
- ....
- ....

☐ I read my Monthly Declarations

To-Do's:

☐ ....
☐ ....
☐ ....
☐ ....
☐ ....

People to Contact:

☐ ....
☐ ....
☐ ....
☐ ....
☐ ....

Expenses: Investing/ Saving:

Item	Amount	Item	Amount

DAILY TRACKER

Date ....

Intention: ....
....

Affirmation: ....
....

Word of the Day: ....

7 :00	
:30	
8 :00	
:30	
9 :00	
:30	
10 :00	
:30	
11 :00	
:30	
12 :00	
:30	
1 :00	
:30	
2 :00	
:30	
3 :00	
:30	
4 :00	
:30	
5 :00	
:30	
6 :00	
:30	
7 :00	
:30	
8 :00	
:30	
9 :00	
:30	
10 :00	
:30	

- Exercise/Stretches: .... mins
- Pray/Meditation: .... mins
- Read/Audio: .... mins

I am reading /listening to:

_____

I Am Grateful for:

- ....
- ....
- ....
- ....
- ....

☐ I read my Monthly Declarations

To-Do's:

☐ ....
☐ ....
☐ ....
☐ ....
☐ ....

People to Contact:

☐ ....
☐ ....
☐ ....
☐ ....
☐ ....

Expenses: Investing/ Saving:

Item	Amount	Item	Amount

✦ DAILY TRACKER ✦

Date ....

Intention: ....

Affirmation: ....

Word of the Day: ....

7 :00	
:30	
8 :00	
:30	
9 :00	
:30	
10 :00	
:30	
11 :00	
:30	
12 :00	
:30	
1 :00	
:30	
2 :00	
:30	
3 :00	
:30	
4 :00	
:30	
5 :00	
:30	
6 :00	
:30	
7 :00	
:30	
8 :00	
:30	
9 :00	
:30	
10 :00	
:30	

• Exercise/Stretches: .... mins
• Pray/Meditation: .... mins
• Read/Audio: .... mins

I am reading /listening to:

_____

I Am Grateful for:

• ....
• ....
• ....
• ....
• ....

☐ I read my Monthly Declarations

To-Do's:

☐ ....
☐ ....
☐ ....
☐ ....
☐ ....

People to Contact:

☐ ....
☐ ....
☐ ....
☐ ....
☐ ....

Expenses: Investing/ Saving:

Item	Amount	Item	Amount

DAILY TRACKER

Date ....

Intention: ....
....
Affirmation: ....
Word of the Day: ....

7 :00	
:30	
8 :00	
:30	
9 :00	
:30	
10 :00	
:30	
11 :00	
:30	
12 :00	
:30	
1 :00	
:30	
2 :00	
:30	
3 :00	
:30	
4 :00	
:30	
5 :00	
:30	
6 :00	
:30	
7 :00	
:30	
8 :00	
:30	
9 :00	
:30	
10 :00	
:30	

- Exercise/Stretches: .... mins
- Pray/Meditation: .... mins
- Read/Audio: .... mins

I am reading /listening to:

_____

I Am Grateful for:

- ....
- ....
- ....
- ....
- ....

☐ I read my Monthly Declarations

To-Do's:

☐ ....
☐ ....
☐ ....
☐ ....
☐ ....

People to Contact:

☐ ....
☐ ....
☐ ....
☐ ....
☐ ....

Expenses: Investing/ Saving:

Item	Amount	Item	Amount

MONTHLY CHECK-IN

In this section spend quiet time reflecting on your month, what you created, what are some lessons learned, and in what ways are you committed to creating something different.

What's working:

_____
_____
_____
_____
_____
_____
_____
_____
_____
_____
_____

What's not working:

_____
_____
_____
_____
_____
_____
_____
_____

What am I committed to doing differently to create different results?

_____
_____
_____
_____
_____
_____
_____
_____
_____
_____

Month

MONTHLY EXPENSE TRACKER

Date	Expense Category	Budget	Actual
	Donating/Tithing		
	Living Expenses		
	Rent/ Mortgage		
Total		$	$

MONTHLY INCOME & SAVINGS TRACKER

Date	Income	Savings/ Investing	Account
Total	$	$	

MONTHLY NOTES / JOURNAL

MONTHLY DECLARATIONS

What do you want to achieve in all areas of your life this month?

Faith/Spirituality:

- _____
- _____
- _____

Mindset/Personal   Development:

- _____
- _____
- _____

Family/Relationships:

- _____
- _____
- _____

Health/Fitness:

- _____
- _____
- _____

Business/Career:

- _____
- _____
- _____

Community/Contribution:

- _____
- _____
- _____

Money/Finances:

- _____
- _____
- _____

I, *(full name)* _____

declare to accomplish the above handwritten goals in excellence by (date) _____

DAILY TRACKER

Date ....

Intention: ....
....

Affirmation: ....
....

Word of the Day: ....

7	:00	
	:30	
8	:00	
	:30	
9	:00	
	:30	
10	:00	
	:30	
11	:00	
	:30	
12	:00	
	:30	
1	:00	
	:30	
2	:00	
	:30	
3	:00	
	:30	
4	:00	
	:30	
5	:00	
	:30	
6	:00	
	:30	
7	:00	
	:30	
8	:00	
	:30	
9	:00	
	:30	
10	:00	
	:30	

- Exercise/Stretches: .... mins
- Pray/Meditation: .... mins
- Read/Audio: .... mins

I am reading /listening to:
_____

I Am Grateful for:
- ....
- ....
- ....
- ....
-

☐ I read my Monthly Declarations

To-Do's:
☐ ....
☐ ....
☐ ....
☐ ....
☐

People to Contact:
☐ ....
☐ ....
☐ ....
☐ ....
☐

Expenses: Investing/ Saving:

Item	Amount	Item	Amount

DAILY TRACKER

Date ....

Intention: ....
Affirmation: ....
Word of the Day: ....

7 :00	
:30	
8 :00	
:30	
9 :00	
:30	
10 :00	
:30	
11 :00	
:30	
12 :00	
:30	
1 :00	
:30	
2 :00	
:30	
3 :00	
:30	
4 :00	
:30	
5 :00	
:30	
6 :00	
:30	
7 :00	
:30	
8 :00	
:30	
9 :00	
:30	
10 :00	
:30	

- Exercise/Stretches: .... mins
- Pray/Meditation: .... mins
- Read/Audio: .... mins

I am reading /listening to:

_____

I Am Grateful for:

- ....
- ....
- ....
- ....
- ....

☐ I read my Monthly Declarations

To-Do's:
☐ ....
☐ ....
☐ ....
☐ ....
☐ ....

People to Contact:
☐ ....
☐ ....
☐ ....
☐ ....
☐ ....

Expenses: Investing/ Saving:

Item	Amount	Item	Amount

DAILY TRACKER

Date_____

Intention:_____
Affirmation:_____
Word of the Day:_____

7 :00	
:30	
8 :00	
:30	
9 :00	
:30	
10 :00	
:30	
11 :00	
:30	
12 :00	
:30	
1 :00	
:30	
2 :00	
:30	
3 :00	
:30	
4 :00	
:30	
5 :00	
:30	
6 :00	
:30	
7 :00	
:30	
8 :00	
:30	
9 :00	
:30	
10 :00	
:30	

- Exercise/Stretches: _____ mins
- Pray/Meditation: _____ mins
- Read/Audio: _____ mins

I am reading /listening to:
_____

I Am Grateful for:
- _____
- _____
- _____
- _____
- _____

☐ I read my Monthly Declarations

To-Do's:
☐ _____
☐ _____
☐ _____
☐ _____
☐ _____

People to Contact:
☐ _____
☐ _____
☐ _____
☐ _____
☐ _____

Expenses: Investing/ Saving:

Item	Amount	Item	Amount

DAILY TRACKER

Date ....

Intention: ....
Affirmation: ....
Word of the Day: ....

7 :00	
:30	
8 :00	
:30	
9 :00	
:30	
10 :00	
:30	
11 :00	
:30	
12 :00	
:30	
1 :00	
:30	
2 :00	
:30	
3 :00	
:30	
4 :00	
:30	
5 :00	
:30	
6 :00	
:30	
7 :00	
:30	
8 :00	
:30	
9 :00	
:30	
10 :00	
:30	

- Exercise/Stretches: .... mins
- Pray/Meditation: .... mins
- Read/Audio: .... mins

I am reading /listening to:
_____

I Am Grateful for:
- ....
- ....
- ....
- ....
- ....

☐ I read my Monthly Declarations

To-Do's:
☐ ....
☐ ....
☐ ....
☐ ....
☐ ....

People to Contact:
☐ ....
☐ ....
☐ ....
☐ ....
☐ ....

Expenses: Investing/ Saving:

Item	Amount	Item	Amount

DAILY TRACKER

Date ....

Intention: ....

Affirmation: ....

Word of the Day: ....

7 :00	
:30	
8 :00	
:30	
9 :00	
:30	
10 :00	
:30	
11 :00	
:30	
12 :00	
:30	
1 :00	
:30	
2 :00	
:30	
3 :00	
:30	
4 :00	
:30	
5 :00	
:30	
6 :00	
:30	
7 :00	
:30	
8 :00	
:30	
9 :00	
:30	
10 :00	
:30	

- Exercise/Stretches: .... mins
- Pray/Meditation: .... mins
- Read/Audio: .... mins

I am reading /listening to:

_____

I Am Grateful for:

- ....
- ....
- ....
- ....
- ....

☐ I read my Monthly Declarations

To-Do's:

☐ ....
☐ ....
☐ ....
☐ ....
☐ ....

People to Contact:

☐ ....
☐ ....
☐ ....
☐ ....
☐ ....

Expenses: Investing/ Saving:

Item	Amount	Item	Amount

DAILY TRACKER

Date ....

Intention: ....
Affirmation: ....
Word of the Day: ....

7	:00	
	:30	
8	:00	
	:30	
9	:00	
	:30	
10	:00	
	:30	
11	:00	
	:30	
12	:00	
	:30	
1	:00	
	:30	
2	:00	
	:30	
3	:00	
	:30	
4	:00	
	:30	
5	:00	
	:30	
6	:00	
	:30	
7	:00	
	:30	
8	:00	
	:30	
9	:00	
	:30	
10	:00	
	:30	

- Exercise/Stretches: .... mins
- Pray/Meditation: .... mins
- Read/Audio: .... mins

I am reading /listening to:

_____

I Am Grateful for:
- ....
- ....
- ....
- ....
- ....

☐ I read my Monthly Declarations

To-Do's:
☐ ....
☐ ....
☐ ....
☐ ....
☐ ....

People to Contact:
☐ ....
☐ ....
☐ ....
☐ ....
☐ ....

Expenses: Investing/ Saving:

Item	Amount	Item	Amount

DAILY TRACKER

Date ....

Intention: ....
....
Affirmation: ....
Word of the Day: ....

7 :00	
:30	
8 :00	
:30	
9 :00	
:30	
10 :00	
:30	
11 :00	
:30	
12 :00	
:30	
1 :00	
:30	
2 :00	
:30	
3 :00	
:30	
4 :00	
:30	
5 :00	
:30	
6 :00	
:30	
7 :00	
:30	
8 :00	
:30	
9 :00	
:30	
10 :00	
:30	

- Exercise/Stretches: .... mins
- Pray/Meditation: .... mins
- Read/Audio: .... mins

I am reading /listening to:

_____

I Am Grateful for:
- ....
- ....
- ....
- ....
- ....

☐ I read my Monthly Declarations

To-Do's:
☐ ....
☐ ....
☐ ....
☐ ....
☐ ....

People to Contact:
☐ ....
☐ ....
☐ ....
☐ ....
☐ ....

Expenses: Investing/ Saving:

Item	Amount	Item	Amount

❧ DAILY TRACKER ❧

Date ....

Intention: ....

Affirmation: ....

Word of the Day: ....

7 :00	
:30	
8 :00	
:30	
9 :00	
:30	
10 :00	
:30	
11 :00	
:30	
12 :00	
:30	
1 :00	
:30	
2 :00	
:30	
3 :00	
:30	
4 :00	
:30	
5 :00	
:30	
6 :00	
:30	
7 :00	
:30	
8 :00	
:30	
9 :00	
:30	
10 :00	
:30	

• Exercise/Stretches: .... mins
• Pray/Meditation: .... mins
• Read/Audio: .... mins

I am reading /listening to:
_____

I Am Grateful for:
• ....
• ....
• ....
• ....
• ....

☐ I read my Monthly Declarations

To-Do's:
☐ ....
☐ ....
☐ ....
☐ ....
☐ ....

People to Contact:
☐ ....
☐ ....
☐ ....
☐ ....
☐ ....

Expenses: Investing/ Saving:

Item	Amount	Item	Amount

❧ DAILY TRACKER ❧

Date ....

Intention: ....
Affirmation: ....
Word of the Day: ....

7 :00	
:30	
8 :00	
:30	
9 :00	
:30	
10 :00	
:30	
11 :00	
:30	
12 :00	
:30	
1 :00	
:30	
2 :00	
:30	
3 :00	
:30	
4 :00	
:30	
5 :00	
:30	
6 :00	
:30	
7 :00	
:30	
8 :00	
:30	
9 :00	
:30	
10 :00	
:30	

• Exercise/Stretches: .... mins
• Pray/Meditation: .... mins
• Read/Audio: .... mins

I am reading /listening to:

_____

I Am Grateful for:
• ....
• ....
• ....
• ....
• ....

☐ I read my Monthly Declarations

To-Do's:
☐ ....
☐ ....
☐ ....
☐ ....
☐ ....

People to Contact:
☐ ....
☐ ....
☐ ....
☐ ....
☐ ....

Expenses: Investing/ Saving:

Item	Amount	Item	Amount

❧ DAILY TRACKER ❧

Date ....

Intention: ....
Affirmation: ....
Word of the Day: ....

7 :00		
:30		
8 :00		
:30		
9 :00		
:30		
10 :00		
:30		
11 :00		
:30		
12 :00		
:30		
1 :00		
:30		
2 :00		
:30		
3 :00		
:30		
4 :00		
:30		
5 :00		
:30		
6 :00		
:30		
7 :00		
:30		
8 :00		
:30		
9 :00		
:30		
10 :00		
:30		

- Exercise/Stretches: .... mins
- Pray/Meditation: .... mins
- Read/Audio: .... mins

I am reading /listening to:

_____

I Am Grateful for:

- ....
- ....
- ....
- ....
- ....

☐ I read my Monthly Declarations

To-Do's:

☐ ....
☐ ....
☐ ....
☐ ....
☐ ....

People to Contact:

☐ ....
☐ ....
☐ ....
☐ ....
☐ ....

Expenses: Investing/ Saving:

Item	Amount	Item	Amount

⚘ DAILY TRACKER ⚘

Date ....

Intention: ....
....

Affirmation: ....
....

Word of the Day: ....

7 :00	_____
:30	_____
8 :00	_____
:30	_____
9 :00	_____
:30	_____
10 :00	_____
:30	_____
11 :00	_____
:30	_____
12 :00	_____
:30	_____
1 :00	_____
:30	_____
2 :00	_____
:30	_____
3 :00	_____
:30	_____
4 :00	_____
:30	_____
5 :00	_____
:30	_____
6 :00	_____
:30	_____
7 :00	_____
:30	_____
8 :00	_____
:30	_____
9 :00	_____
:30	_____
10 :00	_____
:30	_____

• Exercise/Stretches: .... mins
• Pray/Meditation: .... mins
• Read/Audio: .... mins

I am reading /listening to:

_____

I Am Grateful for:
• ....
• ....
• ....
• ....
• ....

☐ I read my Monthly Declarations

To-Do's:
☐ ....
☐ ....
☐ ....
☐ ....
☐ ....

People to Contact:
☐ ....
☐ ....
☐ ....
☐ ....
☐ ....

Expenses: Investing/ Saving:

Item	Amount	Item	Amount

DAILY TRACKER

Date ....

Intention: ....
Affirmation: ....
Word of the Day: ....

7 :00	
:30	
8 :00	
:30	
9 :00	
:30	
10 :00	
:30	
11 :00	
:30	
12 :00	
:30	
1 :00	
:30	
2 :00	
:30	
3 :00	
:30	
4 :00	
:30	
5 :00	
:30	
6 :00	
:30	
7 :00	
:30	
8 :00	
:30	
9 :00	
:30	
10 :00	
:30	

- Exercise/Stretches: .... mins
- Pray/Meditation: .... mins
- Read/Audio: .... mins

I am reading /listening to:

_____

I Am Grateful for:
- ....
- ....
- ....
- ....
- ....

☐ I read my Monthly Declarations

To-Do's:
☐ ....
☐ ....
☐ ....
☐ ....
☐ ....

People to Contact:
☐ ....
☐ ....
☐ ....
☐ ....
☐ ....

Expenses: Investing/ Saving:

Item	Amount	Item	Amount

DAILY TRACKER

Date_____

Intention:_____
_____
Affirmation:_____
Word of the Day:_____

7 :00	
:30	
8 :00	
:30	
9 :00	
:30	
10 :00	
:30	
11 :00	
:30	
12 :00	
:30	
1 :00	
:30	
2 :00	
:30	
3 :00	
:30	
4 :00	
:30	
5 :00	
:30	
6 :00	
:30	
7 :00	
:30	
8 :00	
:30	
9 :00	
:30	
10 :00	
:30	

• Exercise/Stretches: _____ mins
• Pray/Meditation: _____ mins
• Read/Audio: _____ mins

I am reading /listening to:
_____

I Am Grateful for:
• _____
• _____
• _____
• _____
• _____

☐ I read my Monthly Declarations

To-Do's:
☐ _____
☐ _____
☐ _____
☐ _____
☐ _____

People to Contact:
☐ _____
☐ _____
☐ _____
☐ _____
☐ _____

Expenses: Investing/ Saving:

Item	Amount	Item	Amount

DAILY TRACKER

Date ....

Intention: ....

Affirmation: ....

Word of the Day: ....

7 :00	
:30	
8 :00	
:30	
9 :00	
:30	
10 :00	
:30	
11 :00	
:30	
12 :00	
:30	
1 :00	
:30	
2 :00	
:30	
3 :00	
:30	
4 :00	
:30	
5 :00	
:30	
6 :00	
:30	
7 :00	
:30	
8 :00	
:30	
9 :00	
:30	
10 :00	
:30	

- Exercise/Stretches: .... mins
- Pray/Meditation: .... mins
- Read/Audio: .... mins

I am reading /listening to:

_____

I Am Grateful for:

- ....
- ....
- ....
- ....
- ....

☐ I read my Monthly Declarations

To-Do's:

☐ ....
☐ ....
☐ ....
☐ ....
☐ ....

People to Contact:

☐ ....
☐ ....
☐ ....
☐ ....
☐ ....

Expenses: Investing/ Saving:

Item	Amount	Item	Amount

DAILY TRACKER

Date_____

Intention:_____

Affirmation:_____

Word of the Day:_____

7 :00	
:30	
8 :00	
:30	
9 :00	
:30	
10 :00	
:30	
11 :00	
:30	
12 :00	
:30	
1 :00	
:30	
2 :00	
:30	
3 :00	
:30	
4 :00	
:30	
5 :00	
:30	
6 :00	
:30	
7 :00	
:30	
8 :00	
:30	
9 :00	
:30	
10 :00	
:30	

- Exercise/Stretches: _____ mins
- Pray/Meditation: _____ mins
- Read/Audio: _____ mins

I am reading /listening to:

_____

I Am Grateful for:

- _____
- _____
- _____
- _____
- _____

☐ I read my Monthly Declarations

To-Do's:

☐ _____
☐ _____
☐ _____
☐ _____
☐ _____

People to Contact:

☐ _____
☐ _____
☐ _____
☐ _____
☐ _____

Expenses: Investing/ Saving:

Item	Amount	Item	Amount

DAILY TRACKER

Date...

Intention:..
Affirmation:...
Word of the Day: ....

7 :00	
:30	
8 :00	
:30	
9 :00	
:30	
10 :00	
:30	
11 :00	
:30	
12 :00	
:30	
1 :00	
:30	
2 :00	
:30	
3 :00	
:30	
4 :00	
:30	
5 :00	
:30	
6 :00	
:30	
7 :00	
:30	
8 :00	
:30	
9 :00	
:30	
10 :00	
:30	

• Exercise/Stretches: .... mins
• Pray/Meditation: .... mins
• Read/Audio: .... mins

I am reading /listening to:

_____

I Am Grateful for:

• ....
• ....
• ....
• ....
• ....

☐ I read my Monthly Declarations

To-Do's:

☐ ....
☐ ....
☐ ....
☐ ....
☐ ....

People to Contact:

☐ ....
☐ ....
☐ ....
☐ ....
☐ ....

Expenses: Investing/ Saving:

Item	Amount	Item	Amount

DAILY TRACKER

Date ....

Intention: ....

Affirmation: ....

Word of the Day: ....

7 :00	
:30	
8 :00	
:30	
9 :00	
:30	
10 :00	
:30	
11 :00	
:30	
12 :00	
:30	
1 :00	
:30	
2 :00	
:30	
3 :00	
:30	
4 :00	
:30	
5 :00	
:30	
6 :00	
:30	
7 :00	
:30	
8 :00	
:30	
9 :00	
:30	
10 :00	
:30	

- Exercise/Stretches: .... mins
- Pray/Meditation: .... mins
- Read/Audio: .... mins

I am reading /listening to:

_____

I Am Grateful for:
- ....
- ....
- ....
- ....
- ....

☐ I read my Monthly Declarations

To-Do's:
☐ ....
☐ ....
☐ ....
☐ ....
☐ ....

People to Contact:
☐ ....
☐ ....
☐ ....
☐ ....
☐ ....

Expenses: Investing/ Saving:

Item	Amount	Item	Amount

DAILY TRACKER

Date ....

Intention: ....
Affirmation: ....
Word of the Day: ....

7 :00		
:30		
8 :00		
:30		
9 :00		
:30		
10 :00		
:30		
11 :00		
:30		
12 :00		
:30		
1 :00		
:30		
2 :00		
:30		
3 :00		
:30		
4 :00		
:30		
5 :00		
:30		
6 :00		
:30		
7 :00		
:30		
8 :00		
:30		
9 :00		
:30		
10 :00		
:30		

- Exercise/Stretches: .... mins
- Pray/Meditation: .... mins
- Read/Audio: .... mins

I am reading /listening to:

_____

I Am Grateful for:
- ....
- ....
- ....
- ....
- ....

☐ I read my Monthly Declarations

To-Do's:
☐ ....
☐ ....
☐ ....
☐ ....
☐ ....

People to Contact:
☐ ....
☐ ....
☐ ....
☐ ....
☐ ....

Expenses: Investing/ Saving:

Item	Amount	Item	Amount

DAILY TRACKER

Date ....

Intention: ....

Affirmation: ....

Word of the Day: ....

7 :00	
:30	
8 :00	
:30	
9 :00	
:30	
10 :00	
:30	
11 :00	
:30	
12 :00	
:30	
1 :00	
:30	
2 :00	
:30	
3 :00	
:30	
4 :00	
:30	
5 :00	
:30	
6 :00	
:30	
7 :00	
:30	
8 :00	
:30	
9 :00	
:30	
10 :00	
:30	

• Exercise/Stretches: .... mins
• Pray/Meditation: .... mins
• Read/Audio: .... mins

I am reading /listening to:

_____

I Am Grateful for:

• ....
• ....
• ....
• ....
•

☐ I read my Monthly Declarations

To-Do's:

☐ ....
☐ ....
☐ ....
☐ ....
☐ ....

People to Contact:

☐ ....
☐ ....
☐ ....
☐ ....
☐ ....

Expenses: Investing/ Saving:

Item	Amount	Item	Amount

DAILY TRACKER

Date ....

Intention: ....

Affirmation: ....

Word of the Day: ....

7 :00	
:30	
8 :00	
:30	
9 :00	
:30	
10 :00	
:30	
11 :00	
:30	
12 :00	
:30	
1 :00	
:30	
2 :00	
:30	
3 :00	
:30	
4 :00	
:30	
5 :00	
:30	
6 :00	
:30	
7 :00	
:30	
8 :00	
:30	
9 :00	
:30	
10 :00	
:30	

- Exercise/Stretches: .... mins
- Pray/Meditation: .... mins
- Read/Audio: .... mins

I am reading /listening to:

_____

I Am Grateful for:
- ....
- ....
- ....
- ....
- ....

☐ I read my Monthly Declarations

To-Do's:
☐ ....
☐ ....
☐ ....
☐ ....
☐ ....

People to Contact:
☐ ....
☐ ....
☐ ....
☐ ....
☐ ....

Expenses: Investing/ Saving:

Item	Amount	Item	Amount

❧ DAILY TRACKER ❧

Date ....

Intention: ....
Affirmation: ....
Word of the Day: ....

7 :00	_____
:30	_____
8 :00	_____
:30	_____
9 :00	_____
:30	_____
10 :00	_____
:30	_____
11 :00	_____
:30	_____
12 :00	_____
:30	_____
1 :00	_____
:30	_____
2 :00	_____
:30	_____
3 :00	_____
:30	_____
4 :00	_____
:30	_____
5 :00	_____
:30	_____
6 :00	_____
:30	_____
7 :00	_____
:30	_____
8 :00	_____
:30	_____
9 :00	_____
:30	_____
10 :00	_____
:30	_____

• Exercise/Stretches: .... mins
• Pray/Meditation: .... mins
• Read/Audio: .... mins

I am reading /listening to:
_____

I Am Grateful for:
• ....
• ....
• ....
• ....
• ....

☐ I read my Monthly Declarations

To-Do's:
☐ ....
☐ ....
☐ ....
☐ ....
☐ ....

People to Contact:
☐ ....
☐ ....
☐ ....
☐ ....
☐ ....

Expenses: Investing/ Saving:

Item	Amount	Item	Amount

DAILY TRACKER

Date ....

Intention: ....
Affirmation: ....
Word of the Day: ....

7 :00	
:30	
8 :00	
:30	
9 :00	
:30	
10 :00	
:30	
11 :00	
:30	
12 :00	
:30	
1 :00	
:30	
2 :00	
:30	
3 :00	
:30	
4 :00	
:30	
5 :00	
:30	
6 :00	
:30	
7 :00	
:30	
8 :00	
:30	
9 :00	
:30	
10 :00	
:30	

- Exercise/Stretches: .... mins
- Pray/Meditation: .... mins
- Read/Audio: .... mins

I am reading /listening to:

_____

I Am Grateful for:
- ....
- ....
- ....
- ....
- ....

☐ I read my Monthly Declarations

To-Do's:
☐ ....
☐ ....
☐ ....
☐ ....
☐ ....

People to Contact:
☐ ....
☐ ....
☐ ....
☐ ....
☐ ....

Expenses: Investing/ Saving:

Item	Amount	Item	Amount

❧ DAILY TRACKER ☙

Date _____

Intention: _____
_____

Affirmation: _____
_____

Word of the Day: _____

7 :00	
:30	
8 :00	
:30	
9 :00	
:30	
10 :00	
:30	
11 :00	
:30	
12 :00	
:30	
1 :00	
:30	
2 :00	
:30	
3 :00	
:30	
4 :00	
:30	
5 :00	
:30	
6 :00	
:30	
7 :00	
:30	
8 :00	
:30	
9 :00	
:30	
10 :00	
:30	

- Exercise/Stretches: _____ mins
- Pray/Meditation: _____ mins
- Read/Audio: _____ mins

I am reading /listening to:

_____

I Am Grateful for:
- _____
- _____
- _____
- _____
- _____

☐ I read my Monthly Declarations

To-Do's:
- ☐ _____
- ☐ _____
- ☐ _____
- ☐ _____
- ☐ _____

People to Contact:
- ☐ _____
- ☐ _____
- ☐ _____
- ☐ _____
- ☐ _____

Expenses: Investing/ Saving:

Item	Amount	Item	Amount

DAILY TRACKER

Date ....

Intention: ....
Affirmation: ....
Word of the Day: ....

7 :00	
:30	
8 :00	
:30	
9 :00	
:30	
10 :00	
:30	
11 :00	
:30	
12 :00	
:30	
1 :00	
:30	
2 :00	
:30	
3 :00	
:30	
4 :00	
:30	
5 :00	
:30	
6 :00	
:30	
7 :00	
:30	
8 :00	
:30	
9 :00	
:30	
10 :00	
:30	

- Exercise/Stretches: .... mins
- Pray/Meditation: .... mins
- Read/Audio: .... mins

I am reading /listening to:

_____

I Am Grateful for:
- ....
- ....
- ....
- ....
- ....

☐ I read my Monthly Declarations

To-Do's:
☐ ....
☐ ....
☐ ....
☐ ....
☐ ....

People to Contact:
☐ ....
☐ ....
☐ ....
☐ ....
☐ ....

Expenses: Investing/ Saving:

Item	Amount	Item	Amount

DAILY TRACKER

Date _____

Intention: _____

Affirmation: _____

Word of the Day: _____

7	:00	
	:30	
8	:00	
	:30	
9	:00	
	:30	
10	:00	
	:30	
11	:00	
	:30	
12	:00	
	:30	
1	:00	
	:30	
2	:00	
	:30	
3	:00	
	:30	
4	:00	
	:30	
5	:00	
	:30	
6	:00	
	:30	
7	:00	
	:30	
8	:00	
	:30	
9	:00	
	:30	
10	:00	
	:30	

- Exercise/Stretches: _____ mins
- Pray/Meditation: _____ mins
- Read/Audio: _____ mins

I am reading /listening to:

_____

I Am Grateful for:

- _____
- _____
- _____
- _____
- _____

☐ I read my Monthly Declarations

To-Do's:

☐ _____
☐ _____
☐ _____
☐ _____
☐ _____

People to Contact:

☐ _____
☐ _____
☐ _____
☐ _____
☐ _____

Expenses: Investing/ Saving:

Item	Amount	Item	Amount

DAILY TRACKER

Date ....

Intention: ....

Affirmation: ....

Word of the Day: ....

7 :00	
:30	
8 :00	
:30	
9 :00	
:30	
10 :00	
:30	
11 :00	
:30	
12 :00	
:30	
1 :00	
:30	
2 :00	
:30	
3 :00	
:30	
4 :00	
:30	
5 :00	
:30	
6 :00	
:30	
7 :00	
:30	
8 :00	
:30	
9 :00	
:30	
10 :00	
:30	

- Exercise/Stretches: .... mins
- Pray/Meditation: .... mins
- Read/Audio: .... mins

I am reading /listening to:

_____

I Am Grateful for:

- ....
- ....
- ....
- ....
- ....

☐ I read my Monthly Declarations

To-Do's:

☐ ....
☐ ....
☐ ....
☐ ....
☐ ....

People to Contact:

☐ ....
☐ ....
☐ ....
☐ ....
☐ ....

Expenses: Investing/ Saving:

Item	Amount	Item	Amount

⇜ DAILY TRACKER ⇝

Date ....

Intention: ....
....
Affirmation: ....
....
Word of the Day: ....

7 :00	
:30	
8 :00	
:30	
9 :00	
:30	
10 :00	
:30	
11 :00	
:30	
12 :00	
:30	
1 :00	
:30	
2 :00	
:30	
3 :00	
:30	
4 :00	
:30	
5 :00	
:30	
6 :00	
:30	
7 :00	
:30	
8 :00	
:30	
9 :00	
:30	
10 :00	
:30	

• Exercise/Stretches: .... mins
• Pray/Meditation: .... mins
• Read/Audio: .... mins

I am reading /listening to:

_____

I Am Grateful for:
• ....
• ....
• ....
• ....
• ....

☐ I read my Monthly Declarations

To-Do's:
☐ ....
☐ ....
☐ ....
☐ ....
☐ ....

People to Contact:
☐ ....
☐ ....
☐ ....
☐ ....
☐ ....

Expenses: Investing/ Saving:

Item	Amount	Item	Amount

DAILY TRACKER

Date _____

Intention: _____

Affirmation: _____

Word of the Day: _____

7 :00		
:30		
8 :00		
:30		
9 :00		
:30		
10 :00		
:30		
11 :00		
:30		
12 :00		
:30		
1 :00		
:30		
2 :00		
:30		
3 :00		
:30		
4 :00		
:30		
5 :00		
:30		
6 :00		
:30		
7 :00		
:30		
8 :00		
:30		
9 :00		
:30		
10 :00		
:30		

- Exercise/Stretches: _____ mins
- Pray/Meditation: _____ mins
- Read/Audio: _____ mins

I am reading /listening to:

_____

I Am Grateful for:
- _____
- _____
- _____
- _____
- _____

☐ I read my Monthly Declarations

To-Do's:
- ☐ _____
- ☐ _____
- ☐ _____
- ☐ _____
- ☐ _____

People to Contact:
- ☐ _____
- ☐ _____
- ☐ _____
- ☐ _____
- ☐ _____

Expenses: Investing/ Saving:

Item	Amount	Item	Amount

DAILY TRACKER

Date _____

Intention: _____
_____
Affirmation: _____
Word of the Day: _____

7 :00	
:30	
8 :00	
:30	
9 :00	
:30	
10 :00	
:30	
11 :00	
:30	
12 :00	
:30	
1 :00	
:30	
2 :00	
:30	
3 :00	
:30	
4 :00	
:30	
5 :00	
:30	
6 :00	
:30	
7 :00	
:30	
8 :00	
:30	
9 :00	
:30	
10 :00	
:30	

- Exercise/Stretches: _____ mins
- Pray/Meditation: _____ mins
- Read/Audio: _____ mins

I am reading /listening to:
_____

I Am Grateful for:
- _____
- _____
- _____
- _____
- _____

☐ I read my Monthly Declarations

To-Do's:
☐ _____
☐ _____
☐ _____
☐ _____
☐ _____

People to Contact:
☐ _____
☐ _____
☐ _____
☐ _____
☐ _____

Expenses: Investing/ Saving:

Item	Amount	Item	Amount

DAILY TRACKER

Date ....

Intention: ....

Affirmation: ....

Word of the Day: ....

7 :00	
:30	
8 :00	
:30	
9 :00	
:30	
10 :00	
:30	
11 :00	
:30	
12 :00	
:30	
1 :00	
:30	
2 :00	
:30	
3 :00	
:30	
4 :00	
:30	
5 :00	
:30	
6 :00	
:30	
7 :00	
:30	
8 :00	
:30	
9 :00	
:30	
10 :00	
:30	

- Exercise/Stretches: .... mins
- Pray/Meditation: .... mins
- Read/Audio: .... mins

I am reading /listening to:

_____

I Am Grateful for:

- ....
- ....
- ....
- ....
- ....

☐ I read my Monthly Declarations

To-Do's:

☐ ....
☐ ....
☐ ....
☐ ....
☐ ....

People to Contact:

☐ ....
☐ ....
☐ ....
☐ ....
☐ ....

Expenses: Investing/ Saving:

Item	Amount	Item	Amount

DAILY TRACKER

Date ....

Intention: ....
....
Affirmation: ....
....
Word of the Day: ....
....

7	:00	
	:30	
8	:00	
	:30	
9	:00	
	:30	
10	:00	
	:30	
11	:00	
	:30	
12	:00	
	:30	
1	:00	
	:30	
2	:00	
	:30	
3	:00	
	:30	
4	:00	
	:30	
5	:00	
	:30	
6	:00	
	:30	
7	:00	
	:30	
8	:00	
	:30	
9	:00	
	:30	
10	:00	
	:30	

• Exercise/Stretches: .... mins
• Pray/Meditation: .... mins
• Read/Audio: .... mins

I am reading /listening to:
_____

I Am Grateful for:
• ....
• ....
• ....
• ....
• ....

☐ I read my Monthly Declarations

To-Do's:
☐ ....
☐ ....
☐ ....
☐ ....
☐ ....

People to Contact:
☐ ....
☐ ....
☐ ....
☐ ....
☐ ....

Expenses: Investing/ Saving:

Item	Amount	Item	Amount

MONTHLY CHECK-IN

In this section spend quiet time reflecting on your month, what you created, what are some lessons learned, and in what ways are you committed to creating something different.

What's working:

_____
_____
_____
_____
_____
_____
_____
_____
_____
_____
_____

What's not working:

_____
_____
_____
_____
_____
_____
_____
_____

What am I committed to doing differently to create different results?

_____
_____
_____
_____
_____
_____
_____
_____
_____
_____

ABOUT THE AUTHOR

Beth is a financial educator, coach, author and humanitarian. She brings a feminine, holistic approach to the, sometimes, masculine financial environment. By creating a space of financial wellness and wholeness, she supports people in creating breakthroughs in their relationship with Self & money by releasing limiting beliefs that are in the way from creating abundance and prosperity. Making financial education and planning for the future empowering and exciting, creating positive, tangible results through wealthy and healthy money habits, to begin living a financially conscious life.

Her book series 'Make Money Your Partner' are working journal style books, giving a holistic approach to financial freedom, providing people the space to delve deep into creating financial freedom and peace of mind in an empowering, inspiring, and sustainable way.

bethldana.com

CONTINUE YOUR JOURNEY

30-Day Guide to Financial Wellness & Healing

30-Day Guide to Financial Consciousness & Abundance

30-Day Guide to Financial Alchemy & Freedom